celebrating
CANDY

LEISURE ARTS, INC.

Little Rock, Arkansas

Library of Congress Control Number: 2010923372
ISBN-13: 978-1-60900-004-2

contents

CELEBRATING CANDY

We all love candy, especially when it's a handmade confection fresh from the kitchen. Discover how easy it is to make your own delectable sweets with this collection of 75 best-loved recipes from the Leisure Arts Test Kitchen. There are flavors and textures to please candy lovers of all ages! Enjoy the nostalgia of making your favorite fudge, pralines, or toffee. Prepare a delicious gift of beautiful bonbons or crunchy nut brittle. Create special treats for everyday snacking, for holiday celebrations, and just for kids. The candies of your dreams await your discovery!

SUCCESS WITH CANDY

You can be most successful at making candy when you know a few tips from the pros. Here are some of our favorites.

PREPARATION TIPS

- Be a fair-weather cook! Most candy recipes are best prepared on dry, sunny days; rain or high humidity can affect your results.
- Because timing can be critical in candy-making, gather all your supplies and ingredients ahead of time and organize them for efficient handling. Premeasure ingredients in individual bowls, cups, or bags and set aside until needed.
- When butter is specified, do not substitute light butter or margarine. Especially in chocolate recipes, the water content could cause problems.
- When you need to drizzle icing or melted chocolate and you do not have a decorating bag, use a resealable plastic bag. Fill bag half full, seal, and snip off one corner. Make your first snip small, as you can always cut off more if needed.
- To make cookie or graham cracker crumbs, place crumbled pieces in a food processor or blender and pulse until finely ground. Or place pieces in a heavy-duty resealable plastic food storage bag and crush with a rolling pin.
- Follow recipe directions carefully when mixing or heating. *Fold* means to combine by slowly and gently stirring with an over and under motion. *Blend:* to stir together until well mixed. *Beat:* to mix briskly with a fork, spoon, or electric mixer. *Cream:* to blend together until smooth and creamy. *Whip:* to beat rapidly until air is incorporated into a mixture and volume increases. *Simmer:* to cook mixture until it bubbles gently over medium or low heat. *Boil:* to heat on stovetop until bubbles rise constantly to surface and burst.

SUPPLIES

- Use a timer that counts seconds, so you can anticipate when a minute is about to elapse.
- For accurate readings, test your candy thermometer before each use (see Tests for Candy Making, page 139) and make sure the tip is not touching the bottom of the pan. Read the temperature at eye level.
- Use heavy-gauge pans for even heating.

STORAGE TIPS

- After completely cooling candy, store each kind separately to prevent flavors from blending.
- Store soft candy in an airtight container. Use waxed paper between layers to prevent pieces from sticking together.
- Some candy can be frozen up to six months. Freeze in plastic freezer bags or plastic containers with tight-fitting lids.

MAILING TIPS

- Most candies are suitable for mailing unless melting is a concern. Line a sturdy box with waxed paper, aluminum foil, or plastic wrap. Place a layer of crumpled waxed paper or paper towels in bottom of box. Depending on type of candy, wrap pieces individually or place small amounts in plastic bags.
- Use crumpled waxed paper or paper towels to prevent shifting. Tape box securely closed.

CLASSICS

Fudge, toffee, bonbons...these are the classic candies that we consider favorites. Some are creamy. Some are crunchy. A few are chewy, and others melt in your mouth. But every one of them is bound to please!

Peanut Butter Fudge is a creamy winner in the candy world. Dipping the golden fudge in chocolate and chopped pecans gives it a rich twist.

peanut butter fudge

Butter an 8-inch square pan; set aside.

Butter sides of a medium saucepan. Combine sugars, milk, corn syrup, and salt in pan. Stirring constantly, cook over medium-low heat until sugar dissolves. Using a pastry brush dipped in hot water, wash down any sugar crystals on sides of pan. Attach a candy thermometer to pan, making sure thermometer does not touch bottom of pan.

Increase heat to medium and bring to a boil. Cook, without stirring, until mixture reaches soft-ball stage (approximately 234° to 240°). Test about $1/2$ teaspoon mixture in ice water. Mixture will easily form a ball in ice water but will flatten when held in your hand. Remove from heat. Add marshmallows, peanut butter, and butter; stir until smooth. Stir in vanilla. Beat until fudge thickens and begins to lose its gloss. Pour into prepared pan. Cool completely.

Cut fudge into $1^1/2$-inch squares, then cut in half diagonally to form triangles. Dip one edge of fudge pieces into melted chocolate, then into pecans. Place on waxed paper to let chocolate harden.

Store in an airtight container.

YIELD: 1 pound, 10 ounces fudge or about 50 triangles

1 cup granulated sugar
1 cup firmly packed brown sugar
1 cup evaporated milk
$1/4$ cup light corn syrup
$1/8$ teaspoon salt
1 cup large marshmallows, cut into pieces
$1/2$ cup smooth peanut butter
2 tablespoons butter
1 teaspoon vanilla extract
6 ounces chocolate candy coating, melted
1 cup chopped pecans, finely ground

After dinner, or any time of day—it's always a good time for refreshing mints! These taste just like the ones Grandmother used to make.

old-fashioned mints

In a heavy medium saucepan over medium heat, melt butter. Add 2 cups confectioners sugar and corn syrup; stir until well blended. Stirring constantly, cook about 4 minutes or until mixture comes to a boil. Remove from heat and add remaining $1^3/_4$ cups confectioners sugar; stir about 3 minutes or until mixture thickens. Stir in extracts.

Pour mixture onto a smooth, damp surface; use a spatula to knead mixture until cool enough to handle with lightly greased hands. Continue kneading until very smooth and creamy. Divide mixture in half, wrapping one half in plastic wrap. Tint remaining half red. Using a rolling pin, quickly roll red mixture into a 5 x 18-inch rectangle on plastic wrap. Cover with another piece of plastic wrap. Repeat to roll out white mixture; remove plastic wrap and place white layer over red layer. Beginning at 1 long edge, tightly roll up layers, smoothing any cracks with fingers. Using a serrated knife with a sawing motion, carefully cut roll into $3/_8$-inch slices. Store in an airtight container in a cool place.

YIELD: about 4 dozen mints

$1/_4$ cup butter or margarine

$3^3/_4$ cups confectioners sugar, divided

$1/_3$ cup light corn syrup

$1/_2$ teaspoon peppermint extract

$1/_2$ teaspoon vanilla extract

Red paste food coloring

Astonishingly good, Almond Rocha is crunchy toffee loaded with whole almonds. Its creamy chocolate coating is topped with chopped walnuts.

almond rocha

Lightly butter an 11 x 15-inch jellyroll pan; set aside.

In a heavy saucepan, place remaining butter and sugar. Cook on high heat 5 minutes, stirring constantly. Attach a candy thermometer to pan, making sure thermometer does not touch bottom of pan. Reduce heat to medium. Add almonds and cook, without stirring, until mixture reaches hard-crack stage (approximately 300° to 310°) and turns light golden in color. Test about $1/2$ teaspoon mixture in ice water. Mixture will form brittle threads in ice water and remain brittle when removed from the water. Remove from heat and add vanilla extract. Pour into prepared jellyroll pan, spreading evenly. Let cool a few minutes; sprinkle 1 cup of chocolate chips on top. Spread the melted chocolate evenly. Sprinkle with $1^1/2$ cups walnuts; press nuts into chocolate. Refrigerate until chocolate hardens.

Loosen the edges of candy with a knife and turn over in pan. Bring to room temperature. Heat remaining 1 cup chocolate chips in a microwave at 1 minute intervals on 50% power, stirring after each minute, until chocolate melts. Spread warm chocolate on candy and sprinkle with remaining walnuts; press nuts into chocolate. Refrigerate until chocolate hardens.

Break into pieces. Store in an airtight container in a cool place.

YIELD: about $3^1/2$ pounds candy

1   pound butter (not margarine), at room temperature

2   cups sugar

$1^1/2$ cups whole shelled almonds

1   teaspoon vanilla extract

1   package (16 ounces) semisweet chocolate chips, divided

3   cups finely chopped walnuts, divided

Fudge is always a favorite, whether smooth and silky like our Frosted Sour Cream Fudge or full of crunchy nuts, as in this Buttermilk Fudge.

frosted sour cream fudge

Butter an 8-inch square pan; set aside.

Butter sides of a heavy medium saucepan. Combine sugar, sour cream, and salt; cook over medium-low heat, stirring constantly, until sugar dissolves. Using a pastry brush dipped in hot water, wash down any sugar crystals on sides of pan. Attach candy thermometer to pan, making sure thermometer does not touch bottom of pan.

Increase heat to medium and bring to a boil. Stirring constantly, cook until mixture reaches 232°. Remove from heat and add butter. Beat until fudge thickens and begins to lose its gloss. Pour into prepared pan. Spread melted chocolate on top of fudge. Cool until firm. Cut into 1-inch squares. Store in an airtight container in refrigerator.

YIELD: about 4 dozen pieces fudge

2 cups sugar

1 cup sour cream

2 tablespoons butter or margarine

$1/8$ teaspoon salt

1 cup semisweet chocolate chips, melted

buttermilk fudge

Butter an 8-inch square pan; set aside.

Butter sides of a heavy large saucepan or Dutch oven. Combine first 5 ingredients in pan and cook over medium-low heat, stirring constantly, until butter melts and sugar dissolves. Using a pastry brush dipped in hot water, wash down any sugar crystals on sides of pan. Attach candy thermometer to pan, making sure thermometer does not touch bottom of pan.

Increase heat to medium and bring to a boil. Cook, without stirring, until mixture reaches soft-ball stage (approximately 234° to 240°). Test about $1/2$ teaspoon mixture in ice water. Mixture will easily form a ball in ice water but will flatten when held in your hand. Remove from heat; add vanilla. Do not stir until mixture cools to approximately 200°. Beat until fudge thickens and begins to lose its gloss. Stir in walnuts. Pour into prepared pan. Cool completely. Cut into 1-inch squares. Store in an airtight container in refrigerator.

YIELD: about 4 dozen pieces fudge

2 cups sugar

1 cup buttermilk

$1/2$ cup butter or margarine

1 tablespoon light corn syrup

1 teaspoon baking soda

1 teaspoon vanilla extract

$1/2$ cup chopped walnuts

In a box of chocolates, you never know what you're going to get beneath that fancy coating. But you're in control of these bonbons, which are filled with your choice of three fillings or a nut center.

candy sampler

In a small saucepan, melt 9 ounces desired chocolate over low heat, stirring constantly. In batches, fill bonbon candy mold half full with melted chocolate. Using a small paintbrush, brush chocolate up sides of mold. Place mold in freezer 2 minutes or until chocolate hardens. Spoon about $^1/_2$ teaspoon of desired filling (see below) or place 1 nut into each chocolate shell.

Spoon a small amount of chocolate over filling or nut, making sure edges are sealed. Return to freezer 2 minutes or until chocolate hardens. Invert and press on back of mold to release candies. If desired, decorate candies by melting a contrasting color of chocolate over low heat, stirring constantly. Spoon melted chocolate into a pastry bag fitted with a very small round tip. Pipe chocolate onto each candy. Allow chocolate to harden. Store in an airtight container in a cool, dry place.

YIELD: about 2 dozen $1^1/_8$-inch bonbons

For chocolate filling, combine all ingredients in a small saucepan. Stirring constantly, cook over low heat until smooth. Cover and cool to room temperature. Use in recipe for Candy Sampler.

For coconut filling, combine coconut, sugar, corn syrup, and salt in a small saucepan. Stirring constantly, cook over medium heat 3 to 5 minutes or until sugar dissolves and filling thickens. Remove from heat; stir in coconut extract. Cover and cool to room temperature. Use in recipe for Candy Sampler.

For caramel filling, combine caramels and water in a medium saucepan. Stirring occasionally, cook over medium-low heat until caramels melt. Remove from heat; stir in vanilla. Cover and cool to room temperature. Use in recipe for Candy Sampler.

9 ounces semisweet, white, or milk baking chocolate, chopped (enough for 1 recipe filling)

1 recipe desired filling (recipes follow) or $^1/_2$ cup whole unsalted nuts

Desired chocolate for garnish (optional)

CHOCOLATE FILLING

$^1/_2$ cup semisweet chocolate chips

1 tablespoon whipping cream

2 teaspoons butter or margarine

COCONUT FILLING

$^1/_2$ cup sweetened flaked coconut

$^1/_4$ cup sugar

$^1/_4$ cup light corn syrup

$^1/_8$ teaspoon salt

$^1/_8$ teaspoon coconut extract

CARAMEL FILLING

20 caramel candies

1 tablespoon plus 1 teaspoon water

1 teaspoon vanilla extract

Offering melt-in-your-mouth goodness and a hint of mint, these sweet chocolate pieces will be grabbed up quickly.

hint-of-mint hard candy

Line a 9 x 13-inch baking pan with aluminum foil, extending foil over ends of pan; grease foil. Set aside.

Butter sides of a heavy large saucepan. Combine sugar, corn syrup, cocoa, water, and salt in pan. Stirring constantly, cook over medium-low heat until sugar dissolves. Using a pastry brush dipped in hot water, wash down any sugar crystals on sides of pan. Attach a candy thermometer to pan, making sure thermometer does not touch bottom of pan.

Increase heat to medium and bring to a boil. Cook, without stirring, until mixture reaches soft-crack stage (approximately 270° to 290°). Test about $1/2$ teaspoon mixture in ice water. Mixture will form hard threads in ice water but will soften when removed from the water. Remove from heat and stir in butter and mint extract. Pour into prepared pan. Allow candy to harden.

Use ends of foil to lift candy from pan. Break into pieces. Store in an airtight container.

YIELD: about 1 pound, 7 ounces candy

2 cups sugar

1 cup light corn syrup

$1/2$ cup cocoa

$1/2$ cup water

$1/8$ teaspoon salt

1 tablespoon butter or margarine

1 teaspoon mint extract

Bursting with fudgy flavor, Creamy Chocolate Caramels are too tasty to resist. Individual wrappers make them good for now and later.

creamy chocolate caramels

Line a 9-inch square baking pan with aluminum foil, extending foil over 2 sides of pan; grease foil. Set aside.

Butter sides of a heavy Dutch oven. Combine sugar, $^3/_4$ cup whipping cream, corn syrup, and butter in Dutch oven. Stirring constantly, cook over medium-low heat until sugar dissolves. Add chocolate; stir until melted. Using a pastry brush dipped in hot water, wash down any sugar crystals on sides of pan. Attach a candy thermometer to pan, making sure thermometer does not touch bottom of pan.

Increase heat to medium; continue to stir and bring mixture to a boil. Gradually stir in remaining $^3/_4$ cup whipping cream. Stirring frequently without touching sides of pan, cook until mixture reaches firm-ball stage (approximately 242° to 248°). Test about $^1/_2$ teaspoon mixture in ice water. Mixture will form a firm ball in ice water but will flatten if pressed when removed from the water. Remove from heat and stir in vanilla. Pour mixture into prepared pan. Cool several hours at room temperature.

Use ends of foil to lift candy from pan. Use a lightly oiled heavy knife to cut candy into 1-inch squares. Wrap individually in waxed paper and store in a cool place.

YIELD: about 5 dozen caramels

- 2 cups sugar
- 1$^1/_2$ cups whipping cream, divided
- 1 cup light corn syrup
- $^1/_4$ cup butter
- 4 ounces unsweetened baking chocolate, chopped
- 1 teaspoon vanilla extract

Bourbon Pecan Balls are the kind of candy you'll want to keep around to impress guests. Coated with chocolate, they are a spirited treat.

bourbon pecan balls

Combine pecans and bourbon in an airtight container. Allow to stand at room temperature 48 hours, stirring occasionally.

Line baking sheets with waxed paper; set aside.

In a large bowl, combine butter and vanilla. Stir in nuts. Gradually add confectioners sugar until mixture is stiff. Shape mixture into $3/4$-inch balls. Place on prepared baking sheets; cover tightly with plastic wrap. Chill 1 hour.

Melt baking chocolate and candy coating in the top of a double boiler over hot, not simmering, water. Dip balls into chocolate mixture. Replace on baking sheets. Chill until chocolate hardens. Store in an airtight container in refrigerator.

YIELD: about 10 dozen balls

2 cups chopped pecans

$3/4$ cup bourbon

$1/2$ cup butter or margarine, softened

1 teaspoon vanilla extract

9 to 11 cups confectioners sugar

8 ounces unsweetened baking chocolate, chopped

8 ounces chocolate candy coating, chopped

So irresistible! With a noble heritage dating back to the 1600s, these caramelized candies are packed with rich flavor and crunchy nuts.

pecan pralines

Lightly grease a piece of waxed paper; set aside.

Butter sides of a heavy Dutch oven. Combine sugar and baking soda in pan. Add buttermilk and corn syrup. Stirring constantly, cook over medium-low heat until sugar dissolves. Using a pastry brush dipped in hot water, wash down any sugar crystals on sides of pan. Attach a candy thermometer to pan, making sure thermometer does not touch bottom of pan.

Increase heat to medium and bring to a boil. Cook, stirring constantly, until mixture reaches 210° on thermometer; add butter. Continue stirring and cooking until mixture reaches soft-ball stage (approximately 234° to 240°). Test about $1/2$ teaspoon mixture in ice water. Mixture will easily form a ball in ice water but will flatten when held in your hand. Place pan in 2 inches of cold water in sink. Cool to approximately 140°. Remove from sink. Beat until candy thickens and loses its gloss. Quickly stir in pecans and vanilla. Drop by tablespoonfuls onto prepared waxed paper. Allow pralines to cool completely.

Wrap pralines individually in cellophane or plastic wrap and store in an airtight container.

YIELD: about $2^1/2$ dozen pralines

- 2 cups sugar
- 1 teaspoon baking soda
- 1 cup buttermilk
- 1 tablespoon light corn syrup
- $3/4$ cup butter, cut into small pieces
- 2 cups chopped pecans
- 1 teaspoon vanilla extract

A firmer version of old-fashioned taffy, Taffy Twists are made by pulling the confection into long ropes that are cut into individual pieces.

taffy twists

You will need someone to help you pull this candy.

Keep a 1-quart saucepan warm on very low heat in an oven or on the stove until hot mixture has reached correct temperature. Butter a cool surface for working with candy.

Butter sides of a heavy 3-quart saucepan. Combine sugar, corn syrup, water, butter, and cream of tartar in pan. Stirring constantly, cook over medium-low heat until sugar dissolves. Using a pastry brush dipped in hot water, wash down any sugar crystals on sides of pan. Attach a candy thermometer to pan, making sure thermometer does not touch bottom of pan.

Increase heat to medium and bring mixture to a boil. Cook, without stirring, until mixture reaches upper limits of hard-ball stage (approximately 268°). Test about $1/2$ teaspoon mixture in ice water. Mixture will form a hard ball in ice water and will remain hard when removed from the water. Remove from heat; immediately pour half of candy into warm saucepan. Stir $1/2$ teaspoon vanilla and about $1/8$ teaspoon red or green food coloring into each half of candy. Immediately pour each color of candy onto a cool, buttered surface. Allow to cool enough to handle.

With greased hands, pull candy into a long rope. Fold candy back onto itself, twist, and pull again. Continue the pulling, twisting, and folding motion until candy lightens in color, begins to hold its shape, and is no longer sticky. Using a twisting motion, pull into smaller $1/2$-inch-diameter ropes. Use kitchen scissors to cut ropes into $3/4$-inch-long pieces. Allow pieces to cool completely.

Wrap pieces individually in waxed paper. Store in an airtight container.

YIELD: about $1^1/4$ pounds candy

2 cups sugar
$2/3$ cup light corn syrup
$1/2$ cup water
2 tablespoons butter or margarine
$1/4$ teaspoon cream of tartar
1 teaspoon vanilla extract, divided

Red and green liquid food coloring

Packed with citrus flavor, moist Orange Jelly Candy can be cut in fun shapes and rolled in sugar for an enchanting finish.

orange jelly candy

Line an 8-inch square baking pan with aluminum foil, extending foil over 2 sides of pan; grease foil. Set aside.

In a small saucepan, combine apple juice and fruit pectin. Stir in baking soda (mixture will foam). In a heavy medium saucepan, combine 1 cup sugar and corn syrup. Whisking pectin mixture constantly and stirring sugar mixture constantly, cook both mixtures at the same time over medium-high heat about 5 minutes or until pectin mixture dissolves and sugar mixture comes to a rolling boil. Continuing to stir, slowly pour pectin mixture into sugar mixture. Stirring constantly, continue to boil 4 minutes. Remove from heat and stir in orange extract; tint orange. Pour into prepared pan. Chill about 30 minutes or until firm enough to cut.

Use ends of foil to lift candy from pan. Use wet $1^1/_8$-inch to $1^3/_4$-inch cookie cutters to cut candy into desired shapes. Roll pieces in sugar. Store in single layers between waxed paper in an airtight container in refrigerator.

YIELD: about 4 to 5 dozen pieces

$^3/_4$ cup apple juice

2 packages ($1^3/_4$ ounces each) powdered fruit pectin

$^1/_2$ teaspoon baking soda

1 cup sugar

1 cup light corn syrup

$^1/_2$ teaspoon orange extract

Orange paste food coloring

Sugar

Color your world with Glass Candy! Your choice of flavors and food colorings is wide and wonderful.

glass candy

We used the following food colorings and flavors for our candies: orange (combine red and yellow) with orange extract, yellow with lemon extract, red with cinnamon oil, and green with spearmint or wintergreen oil. Recipe makes one color of candy.

Lightly grease a baking sheet; set aside.

Butter sides of a large saucepan. Combine sugar, water, and cream of tartar in pan. Stirring constantly, cook over medium-low heat until sugar dissolves. Using a pastry brush dipped in hot water, wash down any sugar crystals on sides of pan. Attach a candy thermometer to pan, making sure thermometer does not touch bottom of pan.

Increase heat to medium and bring to a boil. Cook, without stirring, until mixture reaches hard-crack stage (approximately 300° to 310°). Test about 1/2 teaspoon mixture in ice water. Mixture will form brittle threads in ice water and remain brittle when removed from the water. Remove from heat and stir in extract or oil and a few drops of food coloring. Pour mixture onto prepared baking sheet. Cool completely.

Break candy into pieces. Coat pieces in confectioners sugar, shaking off excess. Store in an airtight container.

YIELD: about 1 pound candy

2 cups sugar

1 cup water

1/4 teaspoon cream of tartar

1 tablespoon extract or 1 teaspoon flavored oil

Liquid food coloring

Confectioners sugar

EASY DOES IT

When a candy craving hits, you want satisfaction fast. That's when these recipes come in handy. They're all absolutely delicious, uncomplicated confections that go together with very little time or effort. You'll make them again and again!

For a tempting treat that's "gr-r-reat," simply swirl melted chocolate chips into a mix of vanilla candy coating and extra-crunchy peanut butter. The microwave makes it quick and easy.

crunchy tiger butter

(Recipe was tested in a 1200-watt microwave.) Grease a $10^{1}/_{2}$ x $15^{1}/_{2}$-inch jellyroll pan; set aside.

Place candy coating in a medium microwave-safe bowl. Stirring frequently, microwave on 100% power until candy coating melts. Stir in peanut butter. Spread peanut butter mixture into prepared pan.

Place chocolate chips in a small microwave-safe bowl. Stirring frequently, microwave on 100% power until chocolate melts. Pour chocolate over peanut butter mixture; swirl chocolate with a small spatula or knife. Chill until candy hardens.

Break into pieces. Store in an airtight container in a cool place.

YIELD: about $1 \, ^{1}/_{2}$ pounds candy

1 **pound vanilla candy coating**

$^{1}/_{2}$ **cup extra-crunchy peanut butter**

1 **package (6 ounces) semisweet chocolate chips**

This luxurious indulgence is unbelievably easy to create. You just coat butter crackers with a wealth of rich caramel, semisweet chocolate, and finely chopped pecans.

trillionaire candy

Line a baking sheet with waxed paper; set aside.

In a medium saucepan, combine caramel topping and pecans over medium heat. Stirring constantly, bring to a boil and cook 3 to 5 minutes or until mixture thickens. Remove from heat and allow to cool 5 minutes. Spoon about $1^1/_2$ teaspoonfuls of caramel mixture on top of each cracker. Place on prepared baking sheet and chill 1 hour or until firm.

In a small saucepan, melt chocolate chips over low heat, stirring constantly. Remove from heat. Using tongs, dip the bottom of each cracker in chocolate. Return to baking sheet and chill 1 hour or until chocolate is firm. Store in an airtight container in refrigerator.

YIELD: 3 dozen candies

1 container ($12^1/_2$ ounces) caramel topping

1 cup finely chopped pecans

3 dozen round butter-flavored crackers

1 package (12 ounces) semisweet chocolate chips

TIP: This rich candy is a choice gift when you want to tell someone how much you value his or her friendship. Pack it in a little treasure chest or ornate box tagged with this quote from Shakespeare: "I am wealthy in my friends."

These two treats from the microwave are both loaded with crunch. The golden peanut brittle (top) is chock-full of dry roasted peanuts. The buttery toffee is topped with creamy chocolate and chopped walnuts.

microwave peanut brittle

(Recipe was tested in a 1200-watt microwave.) Grease a baking sheet; set aside.

In a 2-quart microwave-safe bowl, combine sugar and corn syrup. Microwave on 70% power 4 minutes. Stir in peanuts; microwave 4 to 5 minutes longer or until mixture turns light golden. Stir in butter, vanilla, and salt; microwave $1\frac{1}{2}$ minutes. Stir in baking soda (mixture will foam). Quickly pour onto prepared baking sheet and spread. Cool completely.

Break into pieces. Store in an airtight container.

YIELD: about 3 cups candy

- 1 cup sugar
- $\frac{1}{2}$ cup light corn syrup
- 1 cup dry-roasted peanuts
- 1 teaspoon butter or margarine
- 1 teaspoon vanilla extract
- $\frac{1}{2}$ teaspoon salt
- 1 teaspoon baking soda

microwave butter toffee

(Recipe was tested in a 1200-watt microwave.) In a large microwave-safe bowl, combine sugar, butter, water, and corn syrup. Microwave on 70% power 4 minutes; stir. Stirring every 2 minutes, microwave 8 to 10 minutes longer or until mixture thickens and turns golden. Stir in vanilla. Pour mixture into an ungreased 9 x 13-inch baking pan. Sprinkle chocolate chips over hot toffee; spread with a spatula. Before chocolate hardens, sprinkle with walnuts. Cool completely.

Break into pieces. Store in an airtight container.

YIELD: about $1\frac{1}{4}$ pounds candy

- $1\frac{1}{3}$ cups sugar
- 1 cup butter, softened
- 2 tablespoons water
- 1 tablespoon dark corn syrup
- 1 teaspoon vanilla extract
- $\frac{3}{4}$ cup semisweet chocolate chips
- $\frac{2}{3}$ cup chopped walnuts

With colorful candy-coated chocolate pieces peeking out, this creamy fudge will have kids giggling and asking for more. No problem—it's so easy that you won't mind making it often.

no-fail microwave fudge

(Recipe was tested in a 1200-watt microwave.) Butter an 8-inch square baking pan; set aside.

In a large microwave-safe bowl, combine confectioners sugar, cocoa, and salt; stir until well blended. Drop butter into sugar mixture. Microwave on 100% power 1 to 2 minutes or until butter melts. Add milk, stirring until smooth. Microwave on 100% power 1 minute longer. Stir in vanilla and chocolate pieces. Pour into prepared pan. Chill 1 hour or until firm.

Cut into 1-inch squares and store in an airtight container.

YIELD: about 4 dozen pieces fudge

$3^1/_2$ cups confectioners sugar

$^1/_2$ cup cocoa

$^1/_4$ teaspoon salt

$^1/_2$ cup butter or margarine, cut into pieces

$^1/_4$ cup milk

1 tablespoon vanilla extract

1 cup candy-coated chocolate pieces

This classic confection requires only a handful of ingredients and whips up fast in the microwave. In no time, you'll have a chocolaty, marshmallowy delight that's too good to keep to yourself.

microwave rocky road fudge

(Recipe was tested in a 1200-watt microwave.) Line an 8-inch square baking pan with aluminum foil, extending foil over 2 sides of pan; grease foil. Set aside.

In a large microwave-safe bowl, combine confectioners sugar, butter, cocoa, milk, and salt. Microwave on 100% power 2 to 2$\frac{1}{2}$ minutes or until butter is melted. Add pecans, marshmallows, and vanilla; stir until well blended. Pour into prepared pan. Refrigerate about 1 hour or until firm.

Use ends of foil to lift fudge from pan. Cut into 1-inch squares and store in an airtight container.

YIELD: about 4 dozen pieces fudge

4$\frac{1}{2}$ cups confectioners sugar
$\frac{1}{2}$ cup butter or margarine
$\frac{1}{3}$ cup cocoa
$\frac{1}{4}$ cup milk
$\frac{1}{4}$ teaspoon salt
$\frac{1}{2}$ cup chopped pecans
$\frac{1}{2}$ cup miniature marshmallows
1 teaspoon vanilla extract

TIP: Microwave Rocky Road Fudge makes a meaningful gift for anyone who makes your journey through life a little smoother. Present the fudge in a box wrapped with highway map paper and a tag saying, "Friendship makes the rough road smooth."

For a sweet alternative to sugar-loaded treats, this fudge can't be beat! Though not low in calories, the creamy candy is full of rich chocolate flavor and chopped nuts. Pecan halves make a pretty garnish.

sugar-free fudge

Line an 8-inch square baking pan with aluminum foil, extending foil over 2 sides of pan; lightly grease foil. Set aside.

Melt margarine and chocolate over low heat in a small saucepan. Remove from heat and stir in sweetener and vanilla.

Place cream cheese in a bowl and add chocolate mixture; beat until smooth. Stir in chopped nuts and spread into prepared pan. Refrigerate until firm.

Use ends of foil to lift fudge from pan. Cut into 1-inch squares. Garnish, if desired. Store in an airtight container in refrigerator.

YIELD: about 4 dozen pieces fudge

$1/4$ cup diet margarine

2 ounces unsweetened baking chocolate

24 packets of Equal® sweetener

1 teaspoon vanilla extract

1 package (8 ounces) reduced-calorie cream cheese, softened

$1/2$ cup chopped pecans

Garnish: about 4 dozen pecan halves

These quick and delicious pralines really stack up the rich flavor. Using the microwave to cook them is a modern approach to making this old-time favorite candy.

microwave pecan pralines

(Recipe was tested in a 1200-watt microwave.) Line baking sheets with aluminum foil; grease foil. Set aside.

In a 4-quart microwave-safe bowl, combine sugar, pecans, buttermilk, butter, and salt. Microwave, uncovered, at 50% power for 12 minutes, stirring every 4 minutes with a wooden spoon. Stir in baking soda (mixture will foam). Microwave 1 minute longer or until mixture is a caramel color (watch closely to prevent mixture from boiling over bowl). Add vanilla; beat with a wooden spoon about 3 minutes or until mixture begins to thicken. Quickly drop by teaspoonfuls onto prepared baking sheets to form about 2-inch-diameter pralines. Cool competely.

Store in single layers between waxed paper in an airtight container.

YIELD: about $3\frac{1}{2}$ dozen pralines

2 cups sugar
$1\frac{1}{2}$ cups chopped pecans
$\frac{3}{4}$ cup buttermilk
2 teaspoons butter or margarine
$\frac{1}{4}$ teaspoon salt
$\frac{1}{2}$ teaspoon baking soda
1 teaspoon vanilla extract

TIDBIT: This microwave recipe is thoroughly modern, but the praline itself dates back many centuries. It is named for the Comte du Plessis-Praslin (1598-1675), whose French chef Lassagne is credited with inventing this method of sugar-coating nuts.

Candy doesn't get any easier than this. Melt a blend of delectable flavors (chocolate candy coating, semisweet chocolate chips, butterscotch chips, and peanut butter chips). Stir in chunks of toasted pecans. Drop by spoonfuls and let it cool. It's ready when you are!

pecan-chocolate candies

Line a baking sheet with waxed paper; lightly grease paper. Set aside.

Stirring constantly, melt butterscotch chips, peanut butter chips, chocolate chips, and candy coating in a heavy large saucepan over low heat. Stir in pecans. Drop candy by tablespoonfuls onto prepared baking sheet. Allow candies to harden.

Store in an airtight container in a cool place.

YIELD: about 5 dozen candies

- 1 package (12 ounces) butterscotch chips
- 1 package (10 ounces) peanut butter chips
- 1 package (6 ounces) semisweet chocolate chips
- 6 ounces chocolate candy coating
- 2 cups chopped pecans, toasted

TIP: The three flavors used in this candy are big favorites that always taste good together. But since the technique is so easy, why not experiment with other flavors? For example, substitute white chocolate chips for the peanut butter, or use dark chocolate chips instead of semisweet.

With a name like truffles, this candy's got to be good! After all, chocolate truffles have quite a reputation to uphold. The surprise is how easy these are to make in the microwave!

easy truffles

(Recipe was tested in a 1200-watt microwave.) In a medium microwave-safe bowl, microwave chips on 50% power until chips soften, stirring frequently until smooth. Stir in $3/4$ cup confectioners sugar, sour cream, orange zest, salt, and wafer crumbs. Shape mixture into 1-inch balls. Roll in confectioners sugar. Place in candy cups. Store in an airtight container in refrigerator.

YIELD: about 5 dozen truffles

1 package (6 ounces) semisweet chocolate chips

1 cup butterscotch chips

$3/4$ cup confectioners sugar

$1/2$ cup sour cream

2 teaspoons grated orange zest

$1/4$ teaspoon salt

1 package (11 ounces) vanilla wafers, finely crushed

Confectioners sugar

TIDBIT: The term *truffle* today is synonymous with sumptuous balls of velvety chocolate candy, but the original truffles were rare French mushrooms that only wealthy royals could afford. After chocolate-making innovations in the late 1800's led to a tantalizing new candy, the creations were named for the exquisite mushrooms they resembled, thus elevating them to the same revered status.

Peanut butter and chocolate are always a winning combination. This easy candy is made by simply melting semisweet chocolate chips and peanut butter chips and then stirring in peanuts and raisins.

chocolate-peanut butter candies

Place about 5 dozen candy cups on baking sheets; set aside.

Melt chocolate chips and peanut butter chips in a heavy medium saucepan over low heat. Stir in peanuts and raisins. Drop teaspoonfuls of candy into candy cups. Chill 30 minutes or until candy is firm.

Store in an airtight container in a cool place.

YIELD: about 5 dozen candies

1 package (12 ounces) semisweet chocolate chips

1 cup peanut butter chips

1 cup lightly salted peanuts

$1/2$ cup raisins

TIP: Miniature candy cups come in all colors and styles of paper and foil, so they are easy to coordinate with a party theme or gift packaging. They're great for candy that melts not only in your mouth, but also in your hand!

Only have a few minutes? That's okay, because that's all you need to stir up a batch of Crunchy Chocolate Candies. This extra-easy confection combines just two ingredients: crispy rice cereal and chocolate candy coating.

crunchy chocolate candies

Place about 3^1/$_2$ dozen candy cups on baking sheets; set aside.

In a heavy medium saucepan, melt candy coating over low heat. Stir in cereal. Drop tablespoonfuls of candy into candy cups. Chill until chocolate hardens.

Store in an airtight container in refrigerator.

YIELD: about 3^1/$_2$ dozen candies

14 ounces chocolate candy coating

2^1/$_2$ cups crispy rice cereal

TIP: If the simple life is your dream, make sure this candy is in your book of favorite recipes. You might even try some variations using cereals made of different grains, or use multi-grain cereals.

Two luscious layers and loads of pecans and raisins make Chocolate-Butterscotch Candy extra special. Our Never-Fail Divinity always turns out right because we substitute marshmallow creme for egg whites.

chocolate-butterscotch candy

Line a 7 x 11-inch pan with waxed paper; set aside.

In separate small saucepans, melt butterscotch and chocolate chips over low heat, stirring constantly. Remove from heat. Stir raisins into butterscotch chips; spread into prepared pan. Stir pecans into chocolate chips; spread over butterscotch mixture. Allow candy to harden.

Cut into 1-inch squares. Store in an airtight container in a cool, dry place.

YIELD: about 5 dozen pieces candy

1 package (11 ounces) butterscotch chips
1 package (12 ounces) semisweet chocolate chips
$1/2$ cup raisins
$1/2$ cup chopped pecans

never-fail divinity

Place marshmallow creme in a large bowl; set aside.

In a large saucepan, combine sugar, water, corn syrup, and salt. Attach a candy thermometer to pan, making sure thermometer does not touch bottom of pan.

Cook over medium-high heat to hard-ball stage (approximately 250° to 268°). Test about $1/2$ teaspoon mixture in ice water. Mixture will form a hard ball in ice water and will remain hard when removed from the water. Beating constantly, gradually add hot mixture to marshmallow creme. Beat until stiff peaks form. Beat in vanilla and pecans. Quickly drop by heaping teaspoonfuls onto waxed paper. Store in an airtight container.

YIELD: about 2 dozen pieces divinity

1 jar (7 ounces) marshmallow creme
$1^1/2$ cups sugar
$1/2$ cup water
2 tablespoons light corn syrup
$1/8$ teaspoon salt
$1^1/2$ teaspoons vanilla extract
1 cup chopped pecans

KIDSTUFF

Kids are wild about candy of all kinds, but they have their favorites, too—like fruity lollipops, sparkling sugared gumdrops, candy-coated blends of crunchy flavors, and smooth creams. You'll find lots of kid-pleasing candies in this adventurous recipe collection.

Lollipop, lollipop, oh lolli lollipop! Let your imagination take wing as you choose shapes, colors, and flavorings for homemade suckers that kids will love. They're super easy to make using crushed hard candies that you melt in the oven.

lollipops

Crush pieces of same-color clear, hard candies. Preheat oven to 275°. Place hard plastic lollipop molds on a baking sheet. Fill molds with crushed candy. Bake 8 to 10 minutes or until candy melts. Remove from oven and insert lollipop sticks into candies. Allow candies to cool. Gently press backs of molds to release candies.

Store in single layers between waxed paper in an airtight container.

TIP: There are dozens of shapes of candy molds to be found, made of various materials. For this recipe, just be sure you use molds that are oven-safe for the specified temperature. We used plastic molds, but tin or aluminum molds are another possibility.

What would mothers do without peanut butter and jelly, because kids sure do love them! Topped with strawberry preserves and a layer of melted peanut butter baking chips, this creamy candy is easy to make and keep on hand in the refrigerator.

peanut butter and jelly fudge

(Recipe was tested in a 1200-watt microwave.) Line a 9 x 13-inch baking pan with a double layer of aluminum foil, extending foil over ends of pan; grease foil. Set aside.

In a large bowl, combine confectioners sugar, cracker crumbs, peanut butter, and butter; stir until well blended. Press mixture into prepared pan.

For topping, place peanut butter chips in a small microwave-safe bowl. Microwave on 100% power 1 minute; stir. Continue to microwave until chips begin to melt, stirring every 15 seconds. Stir until smooth. Spread melted chips over peanut butter mixture.

Use ends of foil to lift fudge from pan; spread preserves over melted chips. Cut into 1-inch squares. Store in an airtight container in refrigerator.

YIELD: about 8 dozen pieces fudge

4$\frac{1}{2}$ cups confectioners sugar

2 cups graham cracker crumbs

1 cup creamy peanut butter

1 cup butter or margarine, melted

1 package (10 ounces) peanut butter chips

$\frac{1}{3}$ cup strawberry preserves

Two sweet treats in one, Microwave Gumdrop Fudge combines chocolaty goodness with chewy gumdrops. The candy cooks in less than 10 minutes, so it's perfect for spur-of-the-moment treats.

microwave gumdrop fudge

(Recipe was tested in a 1200-watt microwave.) Line a 9 x 13-inch baking pan with aluminum foil, extending foil over ends of pan; grease foil. Set aside.

Place butter in a large microwave-safe bowl; microwave on 100% power 1 minute or until butter melts. Stir in confectioners sugar, evaporated milk, and cocoa; microwave on high power (100%) 4 minutes or until mixture comes to a boil, stirring every 2 minutes. Continue to microwave 4 more minutes, stirring every 2 minutes. Add chocolate chips, marshmallow creme, vanilla, and salt; stir until well blended. Stir in gumdrops. Pour into prepared pan. Refrigerate 1 hour or until firm.

Use ends of foil to lift fudge from pan. Cut into 1-inch squares with a lightly oiled knife. Store in an airtight container in a cool place.

YIELD: about 8 dozen pieces fudge

$^{1}/_{2}$ cup butter or margarine

$3^{1}/_{2}$ cups confectioners sugar

1 can (5 ounces) evaporated milk

$^{1}/_{3}$ cup cocoa

1 package (11.5 ounces) milk chocolate chips

1 jar (7 ounces) marshmallow creme

2 teaspoons vanilla extract

$^{1}/_{4}$ teaspoon salt

1 cup small gumdrops

Crunchy AND chewy, this candy packs a double pleasure. Its traditional brittle recipe substitutes colorful jelly beans for the usual peanuts, making it a sure favorite with kids.

jelly bean brittle

Spread jelly beans evenly on greased aluminum foil; set aside.

Butter sides of a large stockpot. Combine next 3 ingredients over medium-low heat; stir constantly until sugar dissolves. Using a pastry brush dipped in hot water, wash down any sugar crystals on sides of pot. Attach candy thermometer to pot, making sure thermometer does not touch bottom of pot.

Increase heat to medium and bring to a boil. Cook, without stirring, until mixture reaches hard-crack stage (approximately 300° to 310°) and turns golden brown. Test about $1/2$ teaspoon mixture in ice water. Mixture should form brittle threads in ice water and remain brittle when removed from the water. Remove from heat and add butter and salt; stir until butter melts. Add soda (mixture will foam); stir until soda dissolves. Pour mixture over jelly beans. Using 2 greased spoons, pull edges of warm candy until stretched thin. Cool completely on foil.

Break into pieces. Store in an airtight container.

YIELD: about 2 pounds brittle

$1^1/_2$ cups jelly beans
3 cups sugar
1 cup light corn syrup
$^1/_2$ cup water
3 tablespoons butter or margarine
1 teaspoon salt
2 teaspoons baking soda

What's black and white and absolutely delicious? These candies made by combining melted white chocolate with the crumbs of coarsely chopped sandwich cookies. Nestled in individual candy cups, they're easy to serve at parties.

cookies and cream candies

Place about 5½ dozen paper candy cups on baking sheets; set aside.

Melt candy coating in the top of a double boiler over hot, not simmering, water. Reserving 3 tablespoons cookie crumbs to sprinkle on top of candies, fold remaining cookie pieces into melted candy coating. Drop rounded teaspoonfuls of mixture into candy cups. Finely crush reserved cookie crumbs and sprinkle over candies before candy coating hardens. Chill about 15 minutes or until candy coating hardens.

Store in an airtight container in a cool place.

YIELD: about 5½ dozen candies

1 package (24 ounces) vanilla candy coating

26 chocolate sandwich cookies, coarsely chopped

TIP: For delicious taste, you can't go wrong with this traditional chocolate and vanilla combination. But if you are feeling creative, add some paste food coloring to the melted confection to coordinate with a party theme, or use pieces of other-flavored sandwich cookies.

Pink rules! Tinted with strawberry gelatin, this fluffy divinity will be a big hit with girly girls. Bright cupcake cups are a sweet way to pass out these treats.

strawberry divinity

Line a 9-inch square baking pan with aluminum foil, extending foil over 2 sides of pan; grease foil. Set aside.

In a large bowl, use a heavy-duty mixer to beat egg whites until stiff. Gradually beat in gelatin until well blended; set aside.

Butter sides of a heavy medium saucepan. Combine sugar, water, and corn syrup in saucepan. Stirring constantly, cook over medium-low heat until sugar dissolves. Using a pastry brush dipped in hot water, wash down any sugar crystals on sides of pan. Attach a candy thermometer to pan, making sure thermometer does not touch bottom of pan.

Increase heat to medium and bring to a boil. Cook, without stirring, until mixture reaches hard-ball stage (approximately 250° to 268°). Test about $1/2$ teaspoon mixture in ice water. Mixture will form a hard ball in ice water and will remain hard when removed from the water.

While beating at high speed, slowly pour hot mixture over egg whites; beat until candy holds its shape. Spread into prepared pan; cool completely.

Cut into 1-inch squares. Store in an airtight container.

YIELD: about 5 dozen pieces divinity

2 egg whites

1 package (3 ounces) strawberry gelatin

3 cups sugar

$3/4$ cup hot water

$3/4$ cup light corn syrup

Even choosy kids are sure to pick one of these candies. The chunky peanut patties offer extra-rich taste and big peanutty crunch, while the chewies present a more delicate choice with pecans and crispy rice cereal.

easy peanut patties

Combine sugar, pudding mix, and evaporated milk in a heavy medium saucepan over medium-high heat. Stirring frequently, bring mixture to a boil. Reduce heat to medium and boil 5 minutes. Remove from heat. Stir in vanilla. Beat 3 minutes or until candy thickens. Stir in peanuts. Drop by tablespoonfuls onto waxed paper. Allow candy to harden.

Store in an airtight container.

YIELD: about 2 dozen candies

$1^1/_2$ cups sugar

1 package (3 ounces) vanilla pudding and pie filling mix (not instant)

$^3/_4$ cup evaporated milk

1 teaspoon vanilla extract

2 cups Spanish peanuts

white chocolate chewies

Heavily butter baking sheets; set aside.

Combine caramels and evaporated milk in the top of a double boiler over simmering water; stir until smooth. Turn off heat; leave caramel mixture over warm water. Stir in pecans and cereal. Drop mixture by teaspoonfuls onto prepared baking sheets. Chill 1 hour.

Melt candy coating and white chocolate in the top of a double boiler over hot, not simmering, water. Remove from heat. Dip candies into chocolate mixture. Return to baking sheet. Chill candies 30 minutes or until chocolate hardens.

Store in an airtight container in a cool place.

YIELD: about 4 dozen candies

1 package (14 ounces) caramels

$^1/_4$ cup evaporated milk

1 cup chopped pecans, toasted

1 cup crispy rice cereal

10 ounces vanilla candy coating, chopped

4 ounces white baking chocolate, chopped

A sprinkling of colorful decorating sugars creates eyecatching sparkles that make this candy irresistible. Just set it out and let the party get started!

confetti candy

Lightly grease a $10^1/2$ x $15^1/2$-inch jellyroll pan; set aside.

Butter sides of a heavy 3-quart saucepan. Combine sugar, corn syrup, and water in saucepan. Stirring constantly, cook over medium-low heat until sugar dissolves. Using a pastry brush dipped in hot water, wash down any sugar crystals on sides of pan. Attach a candy thermometer to pan, making sure thermometer does not touch bottom of pan.

Increase heat to medium and bring to a boil. Cook, without stirring, until mixture reaches hard-crack stage (approximately 300° to 310°). Test about $1/2$ teaspoon mixture in ice water. Mixture will form brittle threads in ice water and will remain brittle when removed from the water. Remove from heat and stir in cotton candy oil. Immediately pour into prepared jellyroll pan. Quickly sprinkle decorating sugars over candy. Allow candy to cool completely.

Break into pieces. Store in an airtight container.

YIELD: about $1^1/4$ pounds candy

2 cups sugar

1 cup light corn syrup

$1/2$ cup water

$1/4$ teaspoon cotton candy-flavored oil (available where candy supplies are sold)

7 teaspoons assorted colors of coarse decorating sugars (we used red, green, yellow, orange, pink, blue, and purple)

This easy candy is just waiting to be custom-made for your next children's party. Use colors and flavorings to coordinate with your decorating theme, or leave them clear as ice. Their sugar coating makes them magical in any color.

gumdrops

In a Dutch oven, soften gelatin in cold water 5 minutes. Stir in boiling water until gelatin dissolves. Stir in sugar and bring mixture to a boil over medium-high heat. Boil 25 minutes, stirring frequently. Pour mixture into four 3 x 5-inch pans. To each pan add $1/4$ teaspoon desired flavoring and desired food coloring (do not add color for clear gumdrops). Stir until combined. Cover and refrigerate pans overnight.

Using a knife dipped in hot water, cut gelatin mixture into $1/2$-inch cubes. Roll in sugar until well coated. Place gumdrops on a piece of waxed paper and allow to sit at room temperature two days to crystallize.

Store in airtight containers.

YIELD: about 16 dozen candies

4 tablespoons (about 6 envelopes) unflavored gelatin

1 cup cold water

$1^1/2$ cups boiling water

4 cups sugar

$1/4$ teaspoon desired flavoring per pan: lemon extract, orange extract, peppermint extract, etc.

1 to 2 drops desired food coloring per pan (recipe tested using purple, green, pink, and blue neon colors)

Sugar

TIP: We made four colors of gumdrops from one batch by using four 3 x 5-inch pans. If you prefer, you can make two colors using two 8 x 8-inch pans, or one color using one 9 x 12-inch pan. When changing pan sizes, you will need to adjust the number of drops of food coloring that you use.

A kid-pleasing, pop-in-your-mouth treat, Porcupine Candies are a jumble of cocoa-flavored rice cereal, chocolate-covered raisins, and slivered almonds. The Peanut Plank Candy is a golden treasure that outshines all others.

porcupine candies

Butter a piece of waxed paper; set aside.

In a large bowl, combine cereal, raisins, and almonds. Combine marshmallows and butter in a large saucepan. Stirring constantly, cook over low heat until smooth. Remove from heat. Stir in vanilla. Pour marshmallow mixture over cereal mixture; stir until well coated. Use greased hands to shape cereal mixture into $1^1/_2$-inch balls. Place on prepared waxed paper; cool completely.

Store in an airtight container in a cool place.

YIELD: about 3 dozen candies

5 cups cocoa-flavored crispy rice cereal
1 cup chocolate-covered raisins
$^1/_2$ cup slivered almonds
3 cups miniature marshmallows
$^1/_4$ cup butter or margarine
$^1/_2$ teaspoon vanilla extract

peanut plank candy

Line a $10^1/_2$ x $15^1/_2$-inch jellyroll pan with aluminum foil, extending foil over ends of pan; grease foil. Set aside.

Butter sides of a heavy Dutch oven. Combine sugar, corn syrup, and whipping cream in pan. Stirring constantly, cook over medium-low heat until sugar dissolves. Using a pastry brush dipped in hot water, wash down any sugar crystals on sides of pan. Attach a candy thermometer to pan, making sure thermometer does not touch bottom of pan.

Continuing to stir constantly, increase heat to medium and bring to a boil. Stir in peanuts. Cook, without stirring, until mixture reaches soft-ball stage (approximately 234° to 240°). Test about $^1/_2$ teaspoon mixture in ice water. Mixture will easily form a ball in ice water but will flatten when held in your hand. Remove from heat and stir in vanilla and baking soda (mixture will foam). Beat about 3 minutes or until candy begins to thicken. Pour into prepared jellyroll pan; cool.

Use foil to lift candy from pan. Cut into 1 x 2-inch pieces. Store in an airtight container.

YIELD: about 6 dozen pieces candy

$3^1/_2$ cups sugar
1 cup dark corn syrup
$^3/_4$ cup whipping cream
5 cups chopped salted peanuts
1 tablespoon vanilla extract
$^1/_2$ teaspoon baking soda

REFINED FLAVORS

Indulge your taste for gourmet treats! These candies offer special ingredients that cater to the discriminating sweet tooth—with champagne and rum, coffee liqueur and toasted pecans, bold fruits and more.

If there's champagne, there must be a celebration going on, right? Actually, the wonderful taste of these pretty chocolates is reason enough to celebrate. One bite reveals tangy bits of apricots that have been marinated in the sparkling wine.

champagne-apricot creams

Marinate apricots in champagne at room temperature 1 hour. Drain apricots; set aside.

Beat butter and confectioners sugar until fluffy. Stir in marinated apricots. Transfer mixture to a small bowl; cover and chill overnight.

Shape chilled mixture into 2-inch balls; place on a baking sheet lined with waxed paper. Refrigerate until firm.

Melt candy coating and chocolate chips in the top of a double boiler over simmering water. Working with only 4 or 5 candies at a time (keep remainder refrigerated), dip the candies into chocolate mixture. Return to refrigerator to allow chocolate to harden.

Melt white chocolate in microwave or in the top of a double boiler over simmering water. Spoon white chocolate into a pastry bag fitted with a small round tip. Pipe decorative lines on tops of candies; allow chocolate to harden. Store in an airtight container in refrigerator.

YIELD: about 26 candies

- 1 package (6 ounces) dried apricots, diced
- 1 cup brut champagne
- 1/2 cup butter, softened
- 2 1/4 cups confectioners sugar
- 8 ounces chocolate candy coating
- 1 package (6 ounces) semisweet chocolate chips
- 2 ounces white baking chocolate

Laced with coffee-flavored liqueur and toasted pecans, Mocha-Nut Fudge Patties are a chocolate lover's dream come true.

mocha-nut fudge patties

Line baking sheets with waxed paper; set aside.

Butter sides of a heavy large saucepan. Combine sugar and salt in saucepan. Add evaporated milk, corn syrup, and 3 tablespoons butter. Stirring constantly, cook over medium-low heat until sugar dissolves. Using a pastry brush dipped in hot water, wash down any sugar crystals on sides of pan. Attach a candy thermometer to pan, making sure thermometer does not touch bottom of pan.

Increase heat to medium and bring to a boil. Cook, without stirring, until mixture reaches soft-ball stage (approximately 234° to 240°). Test about $1/2$ teaspoon mixture in ice water. Mixture will easily form a ball in ice water but will flatten when held in your hand. Remove from heat. Add remaining 3 tablespoons butter, liqueur, and vanilla; do not stir. Place pan in 2 inches of cold water in sink. Cool to approximately 110°. Remove from sink. Add melted chocolate. Beat until fudge thickens and begins to lose its gloss. Stir in pecans. Drop teaspoonfuls of mixture onto prepared baking sheets. Cool completely. Store in an airtight container in a cool place.

YIELD: about 8 dozen candies

4	cups sugar
$1/2$	teaspoon salt
1	cup evaporated milk
$1/3$	cup light corn syrup
6	tablespoons butter, divided
$1/2$	cup coffee-flavored liqueur
2	teaspoons vanilla extract
$1^1/2$	cups semisweet chocolate chips, melted
1	cup finely chopped toasted pecans

A tropical paradise for the taste buds, Hawaiian Fudge is a fruity delight loaded with sun-ripened pineapple, crunchy macadamia nuts, and flaked coconut.

hawaiian fudge

Drain pineapple (do not squeeze dry); reserve juice. Line an 8-inch square baking pan with aluminum foil, extending foil over 2 sides of pan; grease foil. Set aside.

Butter sides of a heavy large saucepan. Combine sugar, whipping cream, pineapple, and 2 tablespoons reserved pineapple juice in saucepan. Stirring constantly, cook over medium-low heat until sugar dissolves. Using a pastry brush dipped in hot water, wash down any sugar crystals on sides of pan. Attach a candy thermometer to pan, making sure thermometer does not touch bottom of pan.

Increase heat to medium and bring to a boil. Cook, without stirring, until mixture reaches soft-ball stage (approximately 234° to 240°). Test about $1/2$ teaspoon mixture in ice water. Mixture will easily form a ball in ice water but will flatten when held in your hand. Place pan in 2 inches of cold water in sink. Add butter and vanilla; do not stir. Cool to approximately 110°. Remove from sink. Beat until fudge thickens and begins to lose its gloss. Stir in macadamia nuts, coconut, and ginger. Pour into prepared pan. Cool completely.

Use ends of foil to lift fudge from pan. Cut into 1-inch squares. Store in an airtight container in refrigerator.

YIELD: about 4 dozen pieces fudge

1 can (15$1/4$ ounces) crushed pineapple in juice

4 cups sugar

1 cup whipping cream

2 tablespoons butter or margarine

1 teaspoon vanilla extract

1 cup chopped macadamia nuts

$1/2$ cup flaked coconut

1 tablespoon chopped crystallized ginger

Millionaire Fudge strikes it rich with caramel and pecans. No one will ever guess how simple the recipe actually is!

millionaire fudge

Butter an 8 x 11$^1/_2$ x 2-inch baking pan; set aside.

In a heavy 2-quart saucepan, combine sugar, marshmallows, evaporated milk, butter, and salt. Cook over medium heat, stirring constantly, until mixture comes to a boil. Continue cooking and stirring for 5 minutes. Remove from heat. Add chocolate chips and vanilla; stir until chocolate melts. Pour mixture into prepared pan; cool.

In the top of a double boiler over simmering water or in a microwave, melt caramels with water; stir until smooth. Spread over fudge. Lightly press pecans into caramel layer. Allow caramel layer to set before cutting into pieces.

YIELD: about 4 dozen pieces fudge

VARIATION: In the top of a double boiler over simmering water or in a microwave, melt 1 cup semisweet chocolate chips. Drizzle melted chocolate over fudge. Allow to set before cutting into pieces.

2 cups sugar

12 regular marshmallows

$^2/_3$ cup evaporated milk

$^1/_2$ cup butter or margarine

$^1/_8$ teaspoon salt

1 package (6 ounces) semisweet chocolate chips

1 teaspoon vanilla extract

1$^1/_2$ packages (14 ounces each) caramels

2 teaspoons water

1$^1/_2$ cups pecan halves

Dainty little candy cups and a coating of chopped almonds give these creamy White Chocolate Truffles a sweet presentation. For extra flavor, add a touch of créme de cacao liqueur.

white chocolate truffles

Melt chocolate and butter in the top of a double boiler over low heat, stirring constantly. Remove from heat. Add sugar, egg substitute, and liqueur (if using); beat with an electric mixer until smooth. Transfer mixture to a shallow glass casserole dish. Cover and refrigerate 1 hour.

Shape mixture into 1-inch balls; roll in almonds. Cover and refrigerate at least 8 hours.

Serve truffles in candy cups at room temperature. Store in an airtight container in refrigerator.

YIELD: about 2 dozen truffles

- 8 ounces white baking chocolate, chopped
- 1/4 cup butter
- 1/2 cup confectioners sugar
- 2 tablespoons egg substitute
- 2 tablespoons crème de cacao liqueur, optional
- 1 cup slivered almonds, chopped

TIP: We chose a fun, colorful print for these candy cups, making them delightfully dainty for a casual occasion. For a more formal occasion, choose cups made of elegant foil or other fancy papers.

Extra moist with sour cream and honey in the mix, Chocolate Rum Balls are an elegant, tasteful treat. They're rolled in ground chocolate for a richly textured look.

chocolate rum balls

Combine 1 cup chocolate chips, sour cream, honey, and salt in a small saucepan. Stirring constantly, cook over low heat until smooth. Pour into an 8-inch square pan, cover, and freeze 20 minutes.

Shape teaspoonfuls of chocolate mixture into about 36 balls and place on an aluminum foil-covered baking sheet and freeze 10 minutes.

In a blender or food processor, finely grind remaining 1 cup chocolate chips; set aside.

In a large bowl, combine cracker crumbs, sugar, walnuts, butter, and rum. Press crumb mixture around each chocolate ball, forming 1$\frac{1}{2}$-inch balls. Immediately roll in ground chocolate. Store in an airtight container in refrigerator. Serve chilled.

YIELD: about 3 dozen rum balls

2 cups (one 12-ounce package) semisweet chocolate chips, divided

$\frac{1}{4}$ cup sour cream

1 tablespoon honey

$\frac{1}{4}$ teaspoon salt

1$\frac{3}{4}$ cups graham cracker crumbs

1 cup confectioners sugar

$\frac{3}{4}$ cup ground walnuts

$\frac{1}{2}$ cup butter or margarine, melted

$\frac{1}{3}$ cup rum

Lemon-Ginger Creams (center) are luscious candies featuring a blend of marshmallows, lemon zest, and crystallized ginger. For a mellow option with bits of nuts, serve creamy Pistachio Candy.

lemon-ginger creams

Place small candy cups on a baking sheet; set aside. Butter sides of a heavy large saucepan. Combine sugar, whipping cream, and corn syrup in saucepan. Stirring constantly, cook over medium-low heat until sugar dissolves. Using a pastry brush dipped in hot water, wash down any sugar crystals on sides of pan. Attach a candy thermometer to pan, making sure thermometer does not touch bottom of pan.

Increase heat to medium and bring to a boil. Cook, without stirring, until mixture reaches soft-ball stage (approximately 234° to 240°). Test about $1/2$ teaspoon mixture in ice water. Mixture will easily form a ball in ice water but will flatten when held in your hand. Remove from heat and stir in marshmallows until melted.

Pour mixture into a medium heat-resistant nonmetallic bowl. Add lemon juice and lemon zest. Beat 10 to 12 minutes or until thickened. Stir in ginger. Spoon mixture into a pastry bag fitted with a large round tip (#12). Pipe candy mixture into candy cups; chill until firm. Store in an airtight container in a cool place.

YIELD: about $3^1/_2$ dozen candies

$1^3/_4$ cups sugar

1 cup whipping cream

$1^1/_2$ tablespoons light corn syrup

$^3/_4$ cup miniature marshmallows

2 tablespoons lemon juice

$^1/_2$ tablespoon grated lemon zest

2 tablespoons finely chopped crystallized ginger

pistachio candy

Lightly grease a candy mold sheet containing $1^3/_8$-inch dia. molds.

In a medium saucepan, combine first 3 ingredients over medium heat and bring mixture to a boil. Continue to boil 5 minutes, stirring constantly. Remove from heat and stir in butter and pistachio flavoring. Tint to desired color. Pour mixture into a medium bowl. Beat at high speed with an electric mixer 4 to 5 minutes or until mixture thickens and is no longer glossy. Fold in pistachios.

Spoon into prepared candy mold. Refrigerate until firm. Remove candies from mold. Wrap each candy in waxed paper or foil candy wrappers. Store in an airtight container in refrigerator.

YIELD: about 4 dozen candies

1 box (3 ounces) vanilla pudding mix (do not use instant)

1 cup sugar

1 can (5 ounces) evaporated milk

2 tablespoons butter or margarine

1 tablespoon pistachio flavoring

Green food coloring

$^1/_2$ cup chopped pistachios

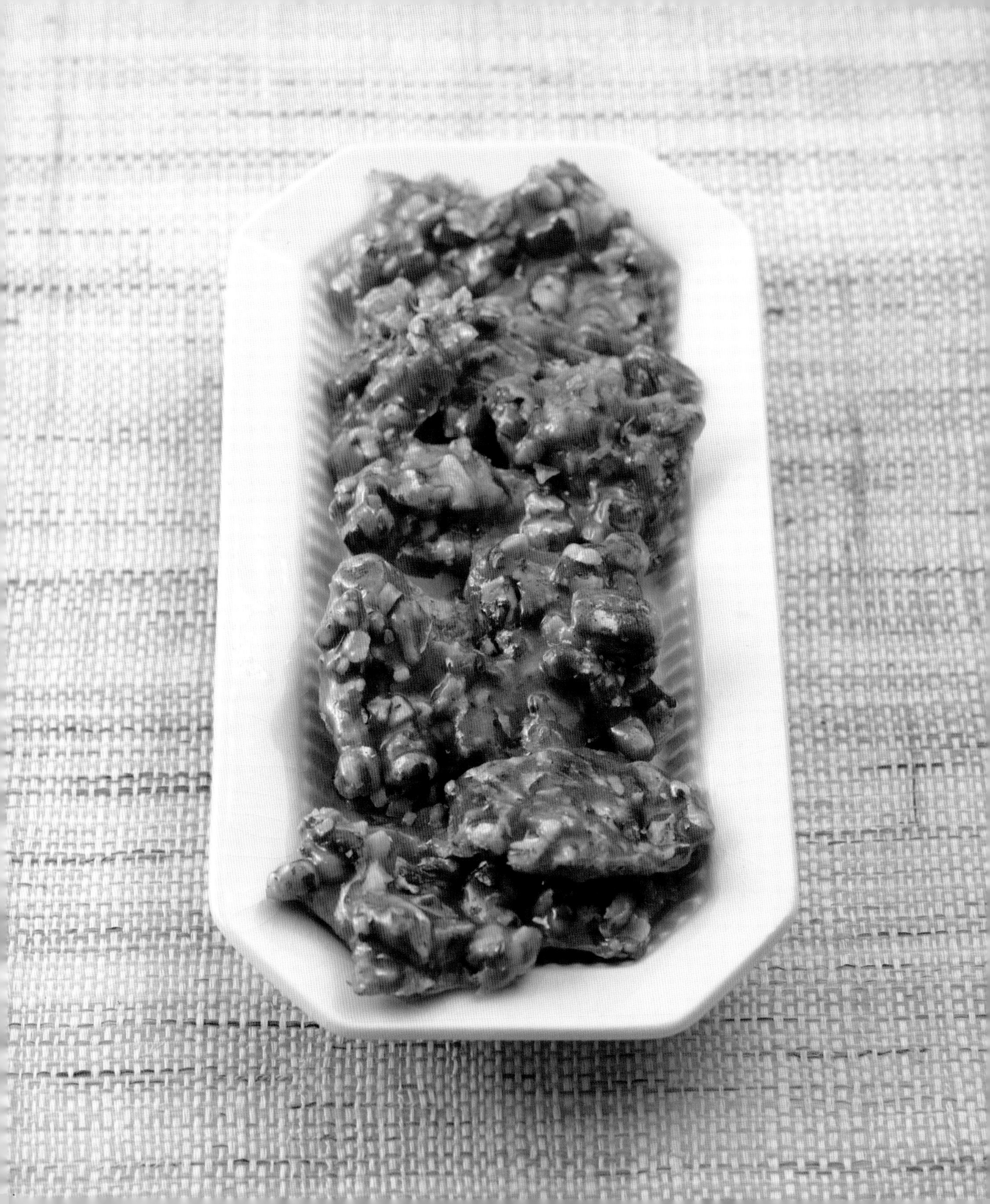

For a taste of distinction, this delicious brittle is packed with toasted pecans. Its golden color gives a hint of the rich flavor you can expect in every bite.

butter-pecan brittle

Butter a large piece of aluminum foil; set aside.

Butter sides of a heavy large saucepan. Combine sugar, corn syrup, and water in saucepan. Stirring constantly, cook over medium-low heat until sugar dissolves. Using a pastry brush dipped in hot water, wash down any sugar crystals on sides of pan. Attach a candy thermometer to pan, making sure thermometer does not touch bottom of pan.

Increase heat to medium and bring to a boil. Cook, without stirring, until mixture reaches hard-crack stage (approximately 300° to 310°) and turns light golden in color. Test about $1/2$ teaspoon mixture in ice water. Mixture will form brittle threads in ice water and will remain brittle when removed from the water. Remove from heat and stir in pecans, butter, vanilla, and salt; stir until butter melts. Add baking soda (syrup will foam); stir until soda dissolves. Pour mixture onto prepared foil. Using a buttered spatula, pull edges of warm candy until stretched thin. Cool completely.

Break brittle into pieces and store in an airtight container.

YIELD: about 2 pounds brittle

2 cups sugar
$3/4$ cup light corn syrup
$1/4$ cup water
3 cups coarsely chopped toasted pecans
$1/4$ cup butter
1 teaspoon vanilla extract
1 teaspoon salt
1 teaspoon baking soda

Finely sliced almonds and a sparkling base make Almond Brittle a delicate surprise. The pieces are so pretty, your guests just might mistake them for art glass…until they hear someone raving about the great taste!

almond brittle

Lightly grease a baking sheet; set aside.

Butter sides of a heavy 3-quart saucepan. Combine sugar and water over medium-low heat. Stir constantly until sugar dissolves. Using a pastry brush dipped in hot water, wash down any sugar crystals on sides of pan. Attach a candy thermometer to pan, making sure thermometer does not touch bottom of pan.

Increase heat to medium and bring to a boil. Cook, without stirring, until mixture reaches hard-crack stage (approximately 300° to 310°) and turns light golden in color. Test about $1/2$ teaspoon mixture in ice water. Mixture will form brittle threads in ice water and will remain brittle when removed from the water. Remove from heat and stir in almonds and extract. Quickly pour mixture onto prepared baking sheet; cool.

Break brittle into bite-size pieces and store in an airtight container.

YIELD: about $1/2$ pound brittle

1 cup sugar
$1/2$ cup water
$2/3$ cup sliced almonds, toasted
$1/2$ teaspoon almond extract

TIP: To toast almonds, spread sliced almonds on an ungreased baking sheet. Stirring occasionally, bake in a preheated 350° oven for 8 to 10 minutes or until nuts are slightly darker in color. Watch carefully to prevent overcooking.

A SWEET YEAR

Holidays give us reasons to celebrate all through the year, and that calls for lots of goodies for entertaining and gift-giving. Surprise your loved ones with valentine sweets, Easter candies, fancy mints for Mom, colorful Halloween treats, and more!

Want a sweet way to spread your love around on Valentine's Day? These heart-shaped confections, created with finely ground almonds and amaretto, are great for lots of little gifts.

marzipan hearts

Lightly spray a candy mold sheet containing $1^1/_8$-inch-wide heart-shaped molds with cooking spray; wipe off excess spray with a paper towel. Set aside.

Process $1^1/_2$ cups confectioners sugar and almonds in a food processor until almonds are finely ground. Add egg whites, amaretto, corn syrup, and orange juice; process until mixture forms a ball. Place ball of almond mixture on a hard surface lightly dusted with confectioners sugar. Knead in additional confectioners sugar as necessary until marzipan is smooth and firm enough to shape.

Divide marzipan in half; tint one half pink. (Work with a small amount of marzipan at a time and keep remaining wrapped in plastic wrap.) Knead small portions of plain and pink marzipan together to create a marbled effect; shape into $3/_4$-inch balls. Press balls into prepared candy molds, shaping into puffy hearts. Remove from molds.

Store hearts in single layers between waxed paper in an airtight container in refrigerator.

YIELD: about 5 dozen hearts

Vegetable oil cooking spray

3 cups confectioners sugar, divided

$1^1/_2$ cups slivered almonds

2 tablespoons pasteurized egg whites

1 tablespoon amaretto

2 teaspoons light corn syrup

1 teaspoon orange juice

Pink paste food coloring

Steal your valentine's heart with this colorful candy! Cherry-Walnut Fudge is loaded with chopped walnuts and candied cherries, and the tiny cherry hearts on top make your gift unforgettable.

cherry-walnut fudge

Line a 7 x 11-inch baking pan with aluminum foil, extending foil over ends of pan; butter foil. Set aside.

Butter sides of a heavy large saucepan. Combine sugar, sour cream, milk, butter, corn syrup, and salt. Stirring constantly, cook over medium-low heat until sugar dissolves. Using a pastry brush dipped in hot water, wash down any sugar crystals on sides of pan. Attach a candy thermometer to pan, making sure thermometer does not touch bottom of pan.

Increase heat to medium and bring to a boil. Cook, without stirring, until mixture reaches soft-ball stage (approximately 234° to 240°). Test about $1/2$ teaspoon mixture in ice water. Mixture will easily form a ball in ice water but will flatten when held in your hand. Place pan in 2 inches of cold water in sink. Add vanilla; do not stir. Cool to approximately 110°. Remove from sink. Beat until fudge thickens and begins to lose its gloss. Stir in walnuts and cherries. Spread mixture into prepared pan. Cool completely.

Use ends of foil to lift fudge from pan. Cut into 1-inch squares. Garnish, if desired. Store in an airtight container in a cool place.

YIELD: about 5 dozen pieces fudge

$2^{1}/_4$ cups sugar
$^{1}/_2$ cup sour cream
$^{1}/_4$ cup milk
2 tablespoons butter or margarine
1 tablespoon light corn syrup
$^{1}/_4$ teaspoon salt
2 teaspoons vanilla extract
1 cup coarsely chopped walnuts
$^{1}/_2$ cup red candied cherries, chopped
Garnish: hearts cut from red candied cherries

For Presidents' Day, celebrate history with these sweet treats that bring to mind the cherry tree George Washington chopped down and the log cabin legacy of Abraham Lincoln. The light and fluffy Cherry Divinity is loaded with bits of candied cherries and walnuts, and the caramel Pecan Logs have a creamy marshmallow center.

cherry divinity

Butter sides of a heavy large saucepan. Combine first 4 ingredients in pan over medium-low heat, stirring constantly until sugar dissolves. Using a pastry brush dipped in hot water, wash down any sugar crystals on sides of pan. Attach candy thermometer to pan, making sure thermometer does not touch bottom of pan.

Increase heat to medium and bring to a boil. Cook, without stirring, until mixture reaches approximately 240°. Using highest speed of an electric mixer, beat egg whites in a large bowl until stiff; set aside.

Continue to cook until mixture reaches hard-ball stage (approximately 250° to 268°). Test about $1/2$ teaspoon mixture in ice water. Mixture will form a hard ball in ice water and will remain hard when removed from the water. While beating egg whites at low speed, slowly pour hot mixture into egg whites. Add vanilla and increase speed of mixer to high. Continue to beat until candy holds its shape. Fold in cherries and walnuts. Drop spoonfuls of divinity onto waxed paper. Store in an airtight container.

YIELD: about 5 dozen pieces divinity

- 2 cups sugar
- $1/2$ cup light corn syrup
- $1/2$ cup water
- $1/8$ teaspoon salt
- 2 egg whites
- 1 teaspoon vanilla extract
- 1 cup chopped red candied cherries
- $1/2$ cup finely chopped walnuts

pecan logs

In a large bowl, stir together confectioners sugar, marshmallow creme, and vanilla. Knead until all the sugar is incorporated. Divide into 6 pieces and shape into 8-inch-long logs. Place in freezer while preparing caramel.

In the top of a double boiler over simmering water or in a microwave, melt caramels with water; stir until smooth. Spoon caramel over each log, then roll in chopped pecans. Refrigerate until set.

Wrap each log in plastic wrap; store in an airtight container in a cool, dry place. To serve, cut each log into $1/2$-inch thick slices.

YIELD: 6 pecan logs

- 4 cups confectioners sugar
- $1/2$ jars (7 ounces each) marshmallow creme (3 cups)
- $1/2$ teaspoons vanilla extract
- 1 package (14 ounces) caramels
- 1 teaspoon water
- 6 cups finely chopped pecans

You don't have to be Irish to indulge in this St. Patrick's Day delight. Creamy Mint Fudge starts out with tinted white chocolate and ends with a topping of satiny semisweet chocolate.

creamy mint fudge

Grease an 8-inch square baking pan; set aside.

Combine white chocolate and sweetened condensed milk in a medium saucepan. Stirring constantly, cook over low heat until chocolate softens. Remove from heat; stir until chocolate melts. Stir in extracts, food coloring, and confectioners sugar. Spread into prepared baking pan. Chill 30 minutes or until firm.

Place chocolate chips in a small microwave-safe bowl. Microwave on 70% power at 1 minute intervals until chocolate softens; stir until smooth. Spread over fudge. Chill 15 minutes or until chocolate hardens.

Cut into 1-inch squares. Store in an airtight container in refrigerator.

YIELD: about 4 dozen pieces fudge

- 2 packages (6 ounces each) white baking chocolate, chopped
- $1/2$ cup sweetened condensed milk
- $1^1/2$ teaspoons vanilla extract
- 1 teaspoon mint extract
- 10 to 15 drops green food coloring
- 1 cup confectioners sugar
- $1/2$ cup semisweet chocolate chips

TIP: Mint is a popular flavor all year, and it doesn't always have to be green. Experiment with different food colors. Pink is especially pretty for lots of occasions.

These charming eggs are definitely the ones you want to find on Easter! Gently speckled in soft spring colors, the White Chocolate Cream Eggs are filled with rich vanilla-pecan nougat.

white chocolate cream eggs

Line baking sheets with waxed paper; set aside.

In a large saucepan, melt butter. Stir in pecans, sugar, milk, and vanilla, blending well. Transfer to a bowl, cover, and chill 2 to 3 hours.

Shape candy mixture into $1^1/_2$-inch-long eggs and place on prepared baking sheets. Cover and refrigerate overnight.

Melt white baking chocolate in the top of a double boiler over medium-low heat. Use a fondue fork to dip candy eggs into melted chocolate. Place on wire racks with waxed paper underneath. Allow chocolate to harden.

To speckle eggs, place a small amount of food coloring on a paper plate. Dilute color with drops of water for a soft look, if desired. Crumple a small square of waxed paper and dip into food coloring; blot on plate. Gently stamp one candy egg to make speckles. Using a paper towel, carefully blot egg to absorb heavy spots of food coloring. Repeat with remaining colors and eggs. Allow eggs to dry, uncovered, in a cool place (do not refrigerate).

YIELD: about $2^1/_2$ dozen candy eggs

$^1/_2$ cup butter or margarine

2 cups finely chopped pecans

3 cups confectioners sugar

$^2/_3$ cup sweetened condensed milk

1 teaspoon vanilla extract

8 ounces white baking chocolate, chopped

Paste food colorings

A tasty combination of chunky peanut butter and semisweet chocolate, these candies are extra pretty for Easter when wrapped in pastel foils. The recipe uses ingredients kept on hand in most kitchens, so you can make them any time.

peanut butter eggs

Line baking sheets with waxed paper; set aside.

In a large bowl, combine sugar, peanut butter, butter, pecans, and vanilla; mix well. Refrigerate until firm, about 1 hour.

Shape heaping teaspoons of mixture into 1-inch-long eggs. Refrigerate 1 hour.

Melt chocolate chips and candy coating in the top of a double boiler over medium-low heat. Use a toothpick to dip eggs in chocolate; place on prepared baking sheets. Allow chocolate to harden.

Store in an airtight container.

YIELD: about 6 dozen eggs

2 cups confectioners sugar

1 cup chunky peanut butter

$\frac{1}{2}$ cup butter or margarine, softened

$\frac{1}{2}$ cup ground pecans

$\frac{1}{2}$ teaspoon vanilla extract

1 package (12 ounces) semisweet chocolate chips

6 ounces chocolate candy coating

TIP: Look for foil candy wrappers wherever candy-making supplies are sold. Besides the obvious places, check the craft stores, too.

Sweeten your Mother's Day gift with a batch of irresistible Cream Cheese Mints shaped like roses or other feminine fancies. Deceptively simple to make, they require no cooking; just mix and press into your choice of candy molds.

cream cheese mints

Beat cream cheese with milk until smooth. Add confectioners sugar, peppermint extract, almond extract, and food coloring; beat until well blended.

Press small amounts of mixture into rose-shaped candy molds. Remove from molds and allow to air-dry at room temperature 4 to 6 hours.

Store in an airtight container.

YIELD: 3 to 4 dozen mints

1 package (3 ounces) cream cheese, softened

1 tablespoon milk

$3\frac{1}{2}$ cups confectioners sugar

$\frac{1}{4}$ teaspoon peppermint extract

$\frac{1}{4}$ teaspoon almond extract

2 or 3 drops red food coloring

TIP: With this simple recipe, you are ready to bring sweetness to any kind of party! The color and shape are totally up to you. How about yellow ducks for a baby shower? Or pale purple posies for a girl's birthday party? Even tiny green frogs to tickle little boys! Have fun!

Dad will love digging into a big bowl of this sweet, crunchy snack on Father's Day (or any day!). The quick and easy mix blends small pretzels with chow mein noodles, golden raisins, peanuts, and a coating of white chocolate.

dad's snack mix

Lightly grease a baking sheet; set aside.

In a large bowl, combine pretzels, raisins, chow mein noodles, and peanuts. In a heavy medium saucepan, melt chips and shortening over low heat. Remove from heat and quickly stir into pretzel mixture. Spread mixture on prepared baking sheet. Refrigerate 10 minutes or until set.

Break candy into bite-size pieces. Store in an airtight container.

YIELD: about $2^3/_4$ pounds of candy

2 cups small pretzels
$1^1/_2$ cups golden raisins
1 cup chow mein noodles
1 cup salted peanuts
1 package (12 ounces) white chocolate chips
1 teaspoon vegetable shortening

TIP: This recipe is extremely versatile. If there's another munchy ingredient Dad loves, throw it in! Give the mix in a tin with a tight-fitting lid so Dad can keep it handy by his favorite chair.

For July Fourth or any all-American occasion, set out a plateful of crunchy toffee topped with red, white, and blue candy coating. Swirling the colors creates a marbleized fireworks effect.

patriotic toffee

Line a 9 x 13-inch baking pan with aluminum foil, extending foil over ends of pan; grease foil. Set aside.

Butter sides of a very heavy large saucepan. Combine sugar, butter, water, and corn syrup in saucepan. Stirring constantly, cook over medium-low heat until sugar dissolves. Using a pastry brush dipped in hot water, wash down any sugar crystals on sides of pan. Attach a candy thermometer to pan, making sure thermometer does not touch bottom of pan.

Increase heat to medium and bring to a boil. Cook, without stirring, until mixture reaches soft-crack stage (approximately 270° to 290°). Test about $^1/_2$ teaspoon mixture in ice water. Mixture will form hard threads in ice water but will soften when removed from the water. Remove from heat and stir in vanilla. Spread mixture into prepared baking pan.

Place candy coating and shortening in a medium microwave-safe bowl. Microwave on 80% power about 3 minutes or until coating melts, stirring after each minute. Place 2 tablespoons melted coating into each of 2 bowls. Tint coating blue and red. Spread remaining white coating over warm toffee. Working quickly before coating hardens, drizzle each tinted coating over toffee (reheating tinted coatings as necessary). Use a table knife to swirl colors through white coating. Gently tap pan on counter to smooth candy surface. Let candy cool.

Use ends of foil to lift toffee from pan; break into pieces. Store in an airtight container.

YIELD: about 1 pound, 7 ounces candy

1 cup sugar

$^3/_4$ cup butter

$^1/_3$ cup water

1 tablespoon light corn syrup

1 teaspoon vanilla extract

12 ounces vanilla candy coating, chopped

$^1/_2$ teaspoon vegetable shortening

Blue and red paste food colorings

Want to play trick or treat with your family and friends on Halloween? Orange Slice Fudge is a delicious treat packed with pieces of orange slice candies, while Jalapeño-Peanut Brittle packs a peppery trick to play on grown-up goblins.

orange slice fudge

(Recipe was tested using a 1200-watt microwave.) Line a 9 x 13-inch baking pan with aluminum foil; grease foil. Set aside. Place butter in a large microwave-safe bowl; microwave on 70% power for 1 minute or until butter melts. Stir in confectioners sugar, evaporated milk, and cocoa. Microwave on 70% power for 4 minutes or until mixture comes to a boil, stirring every 2 minutes. Continue to microwave for 4 minutes longer, stirring every 2 minutes. Add chocolate chips, marshmallows, vanilla, and salt; stir until well blended. Stir in candies. Pour into prepared pan. Refrigerate 4 hours or until firm. Cut into 1-inch squares, cleaning knife frequently. Store in an airtight container in refrigerator.

YIELD: about 8 dozen pieces fudge

- $1/2$ cup butter or margarine
- $3^1/2$ cups confectioners sugar
- 1 can (5 ounces) evaporated milk
- $1/3$ cup cocoa
- 1 package ($11^1/2$ ounces) milk chocolate chips
- 1 package ($10^1/2$ ounces) miniature marshmallows
- 2 teaspoons vanilla extract
- $1/4$ teaspoon salt
- 1 cup chopped orange slice candies

jalapeño-peanut brittle

Butter sides of a heavy large saucepan. Combine sugar, corn syrup, and water in saucepan. Stirring constantly, cook over medium-low heat until sugar dissolves. Using a pastry brush dipped in hot water, wash down any sugar crystals on sides of pan. Attach a candy thermometer to pan, making sure thermometer does not touch bottom of pan.

Increase heat to medium and bring to a boil. Cook, without stirring, until mixture reaches 230° (about 3 minutes). Stir in peanuts and peppers. Stirring occasionally, continue to cook until mixture reaches hard-crack stage (approximately 300° to 310°) and turns golden brown. Test about $1/2$ teaspoon mixture in ice water. Mixture will form brittle threads in ice water and will remain brittle when removed from the water. Remove from heat. Stir in butter, salt, and baking soda (mixture will foam); stir until butter melts. Stir in food coloring. Pour mixture onto greased heavy-duty aluminum foil. Placing 1 rubber spatula on top and a second spatula underneath, lift edges of brittle and stretch as brittle cools. Cool completely; break into pieces. Store in an airtight container.

YIELD: about 1 pound, 9 ounces candy

- $1^1/2$ cups sugar
- $1/2$ cup light corn syrup
- $1/4$ cup water
- 1 can (12 ounces) Spanish peanuts
- $1/4$ cup chopped pickled jalapeño peppers
- $1^1/2$ tablespoons butter or margarine
- $1/2$ teaspoon salt
- 1 teaspoon baking soda
- $1/4$ teaspoon green paste food coloring

So good for autumn celebrations, these caramels are packed with buttery flavor and toasted pecans. It's up to you whether to chew or just let them melt in your mouth.

nutty caramels

Butter a 10½ x 15½-inch jellyroll pan; set aside.

Butter sides of a heavy Dutch oven. Combine sugar, 1 cup whipping cream, corn syrup, and butter in pan. Stirring constantly, cook over medium-low heat until sugar dissolves. Using a pastry brush dipped in hot water, wash down any sugar crystals on sides of pan. Attach a candy thermometer to pan, making sure thermometer does not touch bottom of pan.

Continuing to stir, increase heat to medium and bring to a boil. Gradually add remaining 1 cup whipping cream. Stirring frequently without touching sides of pan, cook until mixture reaches firm-ball stage (approximately 242° to 248°). Test about ½ teaspoon mixture in ice water. Mixture will roll into a firm ball in ice water but will flatten if pressed when removed from the water. Remove from heat and stir in pecans and vanilla. Immediately pour into prepared jellyroll pan. Cool at room temperature several hours.

Cut into 1-inch squares using a lightly oiled heavy knife. Wrap each candy piece in a foil candy wrapper and store in a cool place.

YIELD: about 12½ dozen caramels

2 cups sugar
2 cups whipping cream, divided
1½ cups light corn syrup
¾ cup butter
1½ cups finely chopped toasted pecans
1 teaspoon vanilla extract

This year when you're giving thanks for the good things in life, be sure to include the versatile pumpkin. It adds creamy goodness to this pumpkin pie-spiced fudge.

creamy pumpkin fudge

Line an 8-inch square baking pan with aluminum foil, extending foil over 2 sides of pan; butter foil. Set aside.

Butter sides of a heavy medium saucepan. Combine sugar, evaporated milk, pumpkin, butter, pumpkin pie spice, and salt in saucepan. Stirring constantly, bring mixture to a boil over medium heat; boil 12 minutes. Remove from heat. Add marshmallows, chips, walnuts, and vanilla; stir until marshmallows and chips melt. Pour into prepared pan. Chill until firm.

Use ends of foil to lift fudge from pan. Cut into 1-inch squares. Store in an airtight container in refrigerator.

YIELD: about 4 dozen pieces fudge

$1^{1}/_{2}$ cups sugar

$^{2}/_{3}$ cup evaporated milk

$^{1}/_{2}$ cup canned pumpkin

2 tablespoons butter or margarine

$1^{1}/_{2}$ teaspoons pumpkin pie spice

$^{1}/_{4}$ teaspoon salt

2 cups miniature marshmallows

1 package (12 ounces) white chocolate chips

$^{1}/_{2}$ cup chopped walnuts, toasted

1 teaspoon vanilla extract

CHRISTMAS

The merriest season of the year is famous for its sugarplum fantasies. Is that a coincidence or what! But then, how could it not be merry when so many delicious candies are important traditions? From fudges to peppermints and candied cherries, the recipes in this chapter will fulfill your sweetest Christmas dreams.

Whole maraschino cherries—with stems intact—make an elegant impression when coated with melted white chocolate chips and drizzled with traditional Christmas colors. Make them a few days ahead so the juicy cordial can develop inside.

chocolate-covered cherries

Line baking sheets with waxed paper; set aside.

In a large mixing bowl, combine confectioners sugar, butter, liqueur, milk, and vanilla; chill 1 hour.

Mold a small amount of sugar mixture around each cherry, being careful to completely enclose cherry with mixture. Place on prepared baking sheets; chill 1 hour.

In the top of a double boiler over simmering water, melt white chocolate chips. Dip cherries in white chocolate and return cherries to waxed paper. Allow dipped cherries to sit at room temperature until chocolate hardens.

Check bottoms of cherries and reseal with additional white chocolate, if necessary. Drizzle tops of cherries with melted red and green candy wafers. Cover loosely and store in a cool place at least two days to form cordial (do not refrigerate). Store in an airtight container.

YIELD: about 5 dozen candies

$3^{1}/_2$ cups confectioners sugar

$^{1}/_4$ cup butter or margarine, softened

3 tablespoons crème de cacao liqueur

1 tablespoon milk

1 tablespoon vanilla extract

About 60 maraschino cherries with stems, drained and patted dry

12 ounces white chocolate chips

7 ounces red candy wafers (available where candy making supplies are sold)

7 ounces green candy wafers (available where candy making supplies are sold)

Connoisseurs of confections will love this luscious fudge! Dried cranberries and candied orange peel fill it with Christmas spirit. A hefty chunk in a pretty box makes a sweet party favor.

cranberry-orange fudge

Line an 8-inch square baking pan with aluminum foil, extending foil over 2 sides of pan; grease foil. Set aside.

Combine cranberries and orange juice in a small microwave-safe bowl. Cover and microwave on 100% power 2 minutes, stirring after 1 minute. Allow covered cranberry mixture to stand 10 minutes. Pulse process mixture in a food processor until coarsely chopped; set aside.

Butter sides of a heavy large saucepan. Combine sugar, whipping cream, and corn syrup. Stirring constantly, cook over medium-low heat until sugar dissolves. Using a pastry brush dipped in hot water, wash down any sugar crystals on sides of pan. Attach a candy thermometer to pan, making sure thermometer does not touch bottom of pan.

Increase heat to medium and bring to a boil. Cook, without stirring, until mixture reaches soft-ball stage (approximately 234° to 240°). Test about $1/2$ teaspoon mixture in ice water. Mixture will easily form a ball in ice water but will flatten when held in your hand. Place pan in 2 inches of cold water in sink. Add butter and vanilla; do not stir. Cool to approximately 110°. Remove from sink. Beat until fudge thickens and begins to lose its gloss. Stir in orange peel and cranberries. Pour into prepared pan. Cover and chill 2 hours or until firm.

Use ends of foil to lift fudge from pan. Cut into 1-inch squares, wiping knife clean between cuts. (Fudge is shown cut into 4-inch squares.) Store in an airtight container in refrigerator.

YIELD: about 4 dozen pieces fudge

1 cup sweetened dried cranberries

2 tablespoons orange juice

2 cups sugar

1 cup whipping cream

1 tablespoon light corn syrup

2 tablespoons butter or margarine

1 teaspoon vanilla extract

$1/2$ cup finely chopped candied orange peel

All the goodness of a favorite seasonal beverage is stirred into this remarkably creamy Eggnog Fudge. A touch of brandy extract and freshly grated nutmeg enhance the authentic flavor.

eggnog fudge

Line an 8-inch square baking pan with aluminum foil, extending foil over 2 sides of pan; grease foil. Set aside.

Butter sides of a heavy large saucepan. Combine sugar, whipping cream, corn syrup, and salt in saucepan. Stirring constantly, cook over medium-low heat until sugar dissolves. Using a pastry brush dipped in hot water, wash down any sugar crystals on sides of pan. Attach a candy thermometer to pan, making sure thermometer does not touch bottom of pan.

Increase heat to medium and bring to a boil. Cook, without stirring, until mixture reaches soft-ball stage (approximately 234° to 240°). Test about $1/2$ teaspoon mixture in ice water. Mixture will easily form a ball in ice water but will flatten when held in your hand. Place pan in 2 inches of cold water in sink. Add butter, extracts, and nutmeg; do not stir. Cool to approximately 110°. Remove from sink. Beat about 6 minutes or until fudge thickens and begins to lose its gloss. Pour into prepared pan. Cover and chill about 4 hours or until firm.

Use ends of foil to lift fudge from pan. Cut into 1-inch squares. Store in an airtight container in refrigerator.

YIELD: about 4 dozen pieces fudge

3 cups sugar
$1^1/2$ cups whipping cream
$1/4$ cup light corn syrup
$1/8$ teaspoon salt
2 tablespoons butter
2 teaspoons vanilla extract
$1/2$ teaspoon brandy extract
$3/4$ teaspoon freshly grated nutmeg

Red and green candied cherries add Christmas flair to this creamy candy packed with raisins, pecans, and shredded coconut. The rich taste is sure to sweeten the season!

christmas coconut fudge

Butter a 7 x 11-inch baking pan; set aside.

Butter sides of a medium heavy saucepan. Combine sugar, half and half, corn syrup, and 1 tablespoon butter in pan. Stirring constantly, cook over medium-low heat until sugar dissolves. Using a pastry brush dipped in hot water, wash down any sugar crystals on sides of pan. Attach a candy thermometer to pan, making sure thermometer does not touch bottom of pan.

Increase heat to medium and bring to a boil. Cook, without stirring, until mixture reaches soft-ball stage (approximately 234° to 240°). Test about $1/2$ teaspoon mixture in ice water. Mixture will easily form a ball in ice water but will flatten when held in your hand. Remove from heat and add remaining 1 tablespoon butter; do not stir until mixture cools to approximately 200°. Beat until fudge thickens and begins to lose its gloss. Stir in remaining ingredients. Pour into prepared baking pan. Cool completely.

Cut into 1-inch squares. Store in an airtight container in refrigerator.

YIELD: about 5 dozen pieces fudge

3 cups sugar

$1^{1}/_{4}$ cups half and half

2 tablespoons light corn syrup

2 tablespoons butter or margarine, divided

$1/2$ cup raisins

$1/2$ cup chopped pecans

$1/2$ cup sweetened shredded coconut

$1/2$ cup chopped red and green candied cherries

Fruitcake will gain some new fans when you include these bite-size Fruitcake Mounds in your holiday party fare. They're made simply by coating pieces of prepared fruitcake with melted white chocolate chips. Zesty no-cook Cranberry-Nut Balls are another tasty nibble.

fruitcake mounds

Line baking sheets with waxed paper; set aside.

(Recipe was tested in a 1200-watt microwave.) Place white chocolate chips in a medium microwave-safe bowl. Microwave on 80% power $2^1/2$ minutes or until chips melt, stirring after each minute. Add fruitcake pieces to melted chips; stir until pieces are well coated. Drop teaspoonfuls of mixture onto prepared baking sheets. Chill until chocolate hardens.

Store in an airtight container in a cool place.

YIELD: about 5 dozen candies

2 packages (12 ounces each) white chocolate chips

1 prepared fruitcake (16 ounces), broken into small pieces

cranberry-nut balls

Combine cranberry-orange relish, coconut, and pecans in a medium bowl. Chill 2 hours.

Shape into 1-inch balls (mixture will be sticky). Roll in confectioners sugar. Store in an airtight container in refrigerator.

YIELD: about $3^1/2$ dozen candies

1 cup cranberry-orange relish

1 package (7 ounces) sweetened flaked coconut

1 cup finely chopped pecans

Confectioners sugar

Crushed hard candies add bright colors and fruity flavors to this variation of traditional brittle. The red and green accents make the candy perfect for serving to Christmas guests or for filling holiday gift tins.

"stained glass" brittle

Spread crushed candies evenly in a buttered 10 x 15-inch jellyroll pan; set aside.

Butter sides of a 3-quart heavy saucepan or Dutch oven. Combine sugar, corn syrup, and water in pan. Stirring constantly, cook over medium-low heat until sugar dissolves. Using a pastry brush dipped in hot water, wash down any sugar crystals on sides of pan. Attach a candy thermometer to pan, making sure thermometer does not touch bottom of pan.

Increase heat to medium and bring to a boil. Cook, without stirring, until mixture reaches hard-crack stage (approximately 300° to 310°) and turns light golden in color. Test about $1/2$ teaspoon mixture in ice water. Mixture will form brittle threads in ice water and will remain brittle when removed from the water. Remove from heat and stir in butter and salt; stir until butter melts. Add soda (mixture will foam); stir until soda dissolves. Pour mixture over candies. Using a buttered spatula, spread mixture to edges of pan. Cool completely.

Break into pieces. Store in an airtight container.

YIELD: about $1^1/4$ pounds brittle

$3/4$ cup coarsely crushed red and green fruit-flavored, ring-shaped hard candies

$1^1/2$ cups sugar

$1/2$ cup light corn syrup

$1/4$ cup water

$1^1/2$ tablespoons butter or margarine

$1/2$ teaspoon salt

1 teaspoon baking soda

It's just not Christmas without peppermint and Aunt Marie's divinity! Now you can have both in a single treat. Our easy divinity gets its refreshing minty flavor from crushed peppermint candies.

peppermint divinity

Butter sides of an 8-inch square pan; set aside. Spoon marshmallow creme into a large bowl; set aside.

Butter sides of a heavy medium saucepan. Combine sugar, water, corn syrup, and salt in saucepan. Stirring constantly, cook over medium heat until sugar dissolves. Using a pastry brush dipped in hot water, wash down any sugar crystals on sides of pan. Attach a candy thermometer to pan, making sure thermometer does not touch bottom of pan.

Increase heat to medium-high and bring to a boil. Cook, without stirring, until mixture reaches hard-ball stage (approximately 250° to 268°). Test about $1/2$ teaspoon mixture in ice water. Mixture will form a hard ball in ice water and will remain hard when removed from the water. Remove from heat. While beating with an electric mixer on medium speed, slowly pour hot mixture over marshmallow creme. Add vanilla and increase speed of mixer to high. Continue to beat just until mixture holds its shape. Quickly stir in crushed candies. Press into prepared pan. Allow to harden.

Cut into 1-inch squares. Store in an airtight container.

YIELD: about 4 dozen candies

1 jar (7 ounces) marshmallow creme
2 cups sugar
$1/2$ cup water
2 tablespoons light corn syrup
$1/8$ teaspoon salt
$1/2$ teaspoon vanilla extract
$3/4$ cup finely crushed peppermint candies (about 6 ounces)

While you're decorating this holiday season, dress up your tables with plates of pretty sweets like our Holly Mints. For more luscious mint taste, include a batch of creamy, cool Double Chocolate-Peppermint Crunch.

double chocolate-peppermint crunch

Line an 8-inch square baking pan with aluminum foil, extending foil over 2 sides of pan; grease foil. Set aside.

In the top of a double boiler, combine white baking chocolate and candy coating over hot, not simmering, water; stir until mixture melts. Stir in crushed peppermint candies. Pour mixture into prepared pan. Chill about 20 minutes or until firm.

In a small saucepan, melt bittersweet chocolate over low heat. Spread evenly over candy. Chill about 30 minutes or until chocolate hardens.

Use ends of foil to lift candy from pan. Cut into 1-inch squares. Store in an airtight container in refrigerator.

YIELD: about 4 dozen pieces candy

- 1 **package (6 ounces) white baking chocolate, chopped**
- 6 **ounces vanilla candy coating, chopped**
- $1/2$ **cup finely crushed peppermint candies**
- 4 **ounces bittersweet baking chocolate, chopped**

holly mints

In a large bowl, combine confectioners sugar, butter, evaporated milk, and flavored oil; tint green. Knead mixture until smooth and color is well blended. Firmly press mixture into a $1^1/_2$-inch-long leaf-shaped candy mold. Immediately remove from mold and place on waxed paper. Lightly press cinnamon candies into mints for holly berries.

Store in a cool place in a container with a loose-fitting lid.

YIELD: about 9 dozen mints

TIP: Holly Mints are super festive for the holidays, but the recipe actually can be made in any shape and color you please during the rest of the year. Try pink flower-power shapes with colorful candy sprinkles in the center for summer parties, orange leaves for fall, and so on.

- $4^1/2$ **cups confectioners sugar**
- 5 **tablespoons butter, softened**
- 3 **tablespoons evaporated milk**
- 12 **drops peppermint-flavored oil**
  Green liquid food coloring
  Small red cinnamon candies

Colorful round candies make these cute Christmas tree lollipops extra festive. The whimsical treats are great for kids' parties and for passing out as little gifts for lots of friends.

christmas tree lollipops

Spray a lollipop sheet mold containing $3^{1}/_{2}$-inch-high Christmas tree-shaped molds with cooking spray. Place candies and lollipop sticks in each mold; set aside.

Butter sides of a large heavy saucepan. Combine sugar, water, corn syrup, and butter in saucepan. Stirring constantly, cook over low heat until sugar dissolves.

Increase heat to medium and bring to a boil. Cover and boil 3 minutes. Stir in food coloring. Attach a candy thermometer to pan, making sure thermometer does not touch bottom of pan. Cook, without stirring, until mixture reaches hard-crack stage (approximately 300° to 310°). Test about $^{1}/_{2}$ teaspoon mixture in ice water. Mixture will form brittle threads in ice water and will remain brittle when removed from the water. Remove from heat and stir in flavoring. Spoon into prepared mold in batches, keeping remaining hot mixture in pan over low heat.

As soon as mixture is firm, invert mold onto aluminum foil and press on back to release lollipops. Repeat with remaining candies, lollipop sticks, and hot mixture. Cool lollipops completely.

Wrap each lollipop in plastic wrap.

YIELD: about $1^{1}/_{2}$ dozen lollipops

Vegetable cooking spray

Small, round fruit-flavored decorating candies

Lollipop sticks

2 cups sugar

1 cup water

$^{3}/_{4}$ cup light corn syrup

1 tablespoon butter or margarine

$^{1}/_{4}$ teaspoon green food coloring

$^{1}/_{8}$ teaspoon peppermint- or spearmint-flavored oil

With these colorful candies, you can share some old-fashioned goodness and reminisce about Christmases past. The chewy nougats are packed with walnuts and bits of traditional red and green candied cherries.

old-fashioned candies

Line an 8-inch square baking pan with plastic wrap, extending wrap over 2 sides of pan; set aside.

In a large bowl, combine confectioners sugar, butter, corn syrup, vanilla, and salt; beat until blended. On a flat surface, knead candy until smooth and shiny (about 3 minutes). Knead in cherries and walnuts until evenly distributed. Press candy into prepared pan and smooth with a spatula. Cover and chill overnight in refrigerator.

Use ends of plastic wrap to lift candy from pan. Cut into 1-inch squares. Wrap each piece in waxed paper. Store in refrigerator.

YIELD: about 4 dozen pieces

4 cups confectioners sugar
$1/3$ cup butter, softened
$1/3$ cup light corn syrup
1 teaspoon vanilla extract
$1/8$ teaspoon salt
$1/2$ cup chopped red candied cherries
$1/2$ cup chopped green candied cherries
$1/2$ cup chopped walnuts

TIP: For a different look, use all one color of candied cherries instead of mixing red and green. Candied pineapples offer another color (and taste!) alternative.

KITCHEN TIPS

MEASURING INGREDIENTS

Liquid measuring cups have a rim above the measuring line to keep liquid ingredients from spilling. Nested measuring cups are used to measure dry ingredients, butter, shortening, and peanut butter. Measuring spoons are used for measuring both dry and liquid ingredients.

To measure flour or granulated sugar: Spoon ingredient into nested measuring cup and level off with a knife. Do not pack down with spoon.

To measure confectioners sugar: Sift sugar, spoon lightly into nested measuring cup, and level off with a knife.

To measure brown sugar: Pack sugar into nested measuring cup and level off with a knife. Sugar should hold its shape when removed from cup.

To measure dry ingredients equaling less than $1/4$ cup: Dip measuring spoon into ingredient and level off with a knife.

To measure butter, shortening, or peanut butter: Pack ingredient firmly into nested measuring cup and level off with a knife.

To measure liquids: Use a liquid measuring cup placed on a flat surface. Pour ingredient into cup and check measuring line at eye level.

To measure honey or syrup: For a more accurate measurement, lightly spray measuring cup or spoon with cooking spray before measuring so the liquid will release easily from cup or spoon.

SOFTENING BUTTER OR MARGARINE

To soften butter, remove wrapper from butter and place on a microwave-safe plate. Microwave 1 stick 20 to 30 seconds at medium-low power (30%).

MAKING SUPERFINE SUGAR

Superfine sugar is preferred in some recipes because it dissolves quickly and gives a better texture. Process granulated sugar in a food processor until it becomes a fine powder. Use the same amount as granulated sugar.

SOFTENING CREAM CHEESE

To soften cream cheese, remove wrapper from cream cheese and place on a microwave-safe plate. Microwave 1 to $1^1/2$ minutes at medium power (50%) for an 8-ounce package or 30 to 45 seconds for a 3-ounce package.

TOASTING NUTS

Nuts will stay crisp better and have fuller flavor if toasted before combining with other ingredients. To toast nuts, spread nuts on an ungreased baking sheet. Stirring occasionally, bake 8 to 10 minutes in a preheated 350-degree oven until nuts are slightly darker in color. Watch carefully to prevent overcooking.

PREPARING CITRUS FRUIT ZEST

To remove outer portion of peel (colored part) from citrus fruits, use a fine grater or fruit zester, being careful not to cut into the bitter white portion. Zest is also referred to as grated peel.

TESTS FOR CANDY MAKING

To determine the correct temperature of cooked candy, use a candy thermometer and the cold water test. Before each use, check the accuracy of your candy thermometer by attaching it to the side of a small saucepan of water, making sure thermometer does not touch bottom of pan. Bring water to a boil. Thermometer should register 212 degrees when water begins to boil. If it does not, adjust the temperature range for each candy consistency accordingly.

When using a candy thermometer, insert thermometer into candy mixture, making sure thermometer does not touch bottom of pan. Read temperature at eye level. Cook candy to desired temperature range. Working quickly, drop about $1/2$ teaspoon of candy mixture into a cup of ice water. Use a fresh cup of water for each test. Use the following descriptions to determine if candy has reached the correct consistency:

Soft-Ball Stage (234 to 240 degrees): Candy will easily form a ball in ice water but will flatten when held in your hand.

Firm-Ball Stage (242 to 248 degrees): Candy will form a firm ball in ice water but will flatten if pressed when removed from the water.

Hard-Ball Stage (250 to 268 degrees): Candy will form a hard ball in ice water and will remain hard when removed from the water.

Soft-Crack Stage (270 to 290 degrees): Candy will form hard threads in ice water but will soften when removed from the water.

Hard-Crack Stage (300 to 310 degrees): Candy will form brittle threads in ice water and will remain brittle when removed from the water.

MELTING CANDY COATING

Candy coating, also known as almond bark or chocolate bark, is often preferred over chocolate because it melts easily and isn't soft or tacky at room temperature.

To melt candy coating, place chopped coating in top of a double boiler over hot, not boiling, water or in a heavy saucepan over low heat. Stir occasionally with a dry spoon until coating melts. Remove from heat and use as desired.

To flavor candy coating, add a small amount of flavored oil.

To tint candy coating, use paste food coloring. Add small amounts gradually until desired color is obtained. Do not use liquid food coloring.

To thin, add a small amount of vegetable oil, but no water.

If necessary, coating may be returned to heat to remelt. A way to keep coating warm for dipping candy is to place the pan of melted coating in a larger pan of hot water or in an electric skillet filled with water kept at the "Warm" setting.

USING CHOCOLATE

Chocolate is best stored in a cool, dry place. Since it has a high content of cocoa butter, chocolate may develop a grey film, or "bloom," when temperatures change. This grey film does not affect the taste. When melting chocolate, a low temperature is important to prevent overheating and scorching that will affect flavor and texture. (See *Tempering Chocolate* for more details.)

Make sure your tools and pans are dry. Even the smallest amount of water on your spoon can make chocolate lumpy or cause it to seize.

The following are methods for melting chocolate:

• Chocolate can be melted in a heavy saucepan over low heat, stirring constantly until melted.

• Melting chocolate in a double boiler over hot, not boiling, water is a good method to prevent chocolate from overheating.

• Using a microwave to melt chocolate is fast and convenient. To microwave chocolate, place in a microwave-safe container and microwave, uncovered, on medium-high power (80%) 1 minute; stir with a dry spoon. Continue to microwave 15 seconds at a time, stirring chocolate after each interval until smooth. Frequent stirring is important, as the chocolate will appear not to be melting, but will be soft when stirred. A shiny appearance is another sign that chocolate is melting.

TEMPERING CHOCOLATE

General Information: Tempering chocolate is a method of heating and cooling chocolate that results in a smooth texture and even color for an extended period of time. It is important to use finely chopped chocolate for tempering. Set aside one third of chocolate to add to melted chocolate for cooling. Melt remaining chocolate using double boiler method or microwave method.

When chocolate is completely melted, it should register 88 to 90 degrees for dark chocolate, 85 to 88 degrees for milk chocolate, or 84 to 87 degrees for white chocolate on a candy or chocolate thermometer. To test temper, wipe a thin bit of chocolate onto wax paper and chill 3 minutes. If chocolate is dry to the touch and evenly glossy, it is tempered and ready to use.

Double Boiler Method: Place remaining chocolate in double boiler and, stirring constantly, melt over hot, not simmering, water. As soon as chocolate is melted, remove from heat and add reserved chocolate. If temperature is not low enough, stir until it registers the proper temperature. If chocolate temperature drops too low, rewarm chocolate in double boiler (do not exceed 115 degrees) and then cool to the above temperatures. Retemper as necessary.

Microwave Method: Place remaining chocolate in a microwave-safe glass bowl and microwave on medium power (50%) 1 minute; stir. Microwave 1 minute more; stir until melted. Add reserved chocolate; stir until completely melted. If temperature is not low enough, stir until it reaches the proper temperature. If chocolate temperature drops too low, rewarm chocolate in microwave and then cool until it registers the proper temperature. Retemper as necessary.

IT'S A WRAP

Candy makes wonderful gifts! To present your sweet confections in style, try some of the following gift-wrapping and presentation ideas.

DISHES

Check nearby flea markets, thrift shops, or your own cabinets for one-of-a-kind trays, plates, bowls, cups, sugar bowls, or other mismatched dishes. A pretty piece of floral-pattern china will make your homemade candy look especially irresistible. A vintage sugar bowl or candy dish would be perfect for an assortment of bonbons. Also, inexpensive tins and platters can be found at discount or hobby stores. A sheet of clear or colored cellophane adds a professional finish!

BAGS

Paper bags are handy and quick ways to dress up plastic sackfuls of candy. There are hundreds of beautiful gift bags in all sizes and shapes available at stores everywhere, or you can dress up plain bags with a little bit of paint, colored markers, lace, fabric appliques, beads, buttons, faux flowers, and other craft embellishments. Be creative!

JARS

Jars with tight-fitting lids are great for keeping candy fresh, and they don't have to look ordinary! You can make a simple jar lid cover by placing a pretty handkerchief over the lid and gathering it with a rubber band and a length of ribbon. Or make your own jar skirt by cutting a circle from a piece of fabric. Canning jar rings and lids are easy to embellish; just cut a circle of paper or fabric the same size as the lid. You can even recycle empty glass food jars by cutting and gluing a picture or pretty paper on top of the lid.

GIFT TAGS

No matter what container or theme you choose, don't forget to make a special gift tag. You can use rubber stamps, scraps of fabric and paper, craft foam, and motifs cut from old greeting cards. Scrapbooking supplies are especially nice to use. The possibilities are endless! Add a sprig of greenery or an inexpensive ornament or purse fob for an extra touch.

BASKETS

So easy to tote anywhere, baskets are handy for delivering a gift of sweets. Just line the basket with colorful tissue or a square of cloth and place your bag or jar of candy inside. Tuck in a fancy mug and a tin of flavored coffee mix for a sweet surprise. You can also tie ribbons or scarves to the handles or entwine them with faux flowers.

SPECIAL TOUCHES

Think about ways to personalize your gifts. For book lovers, include their favorite author's latest release along with a box of candy for an indulgent afternoon. For kids, hide the candy inside a new cap or gloves. Please a party host by showing up with a tray laden with ready-to-serve candies in colorful foil cups. For a friend who's just moved into her first apartment, present your candy on a bright and shiny cookie sheet, pizza pan, or other cookware.

metric equivalents

The recipes that appear in this cookbook use the standard United States method for measuring liquid and dry or solid ingredients (teaspoons, tablespoons, and cups). The information on this chart is provided to help cooks outside the U.S. successfully use these recipes. All equivalents are approximate.

METRIC EQUIVALENTS FOR DIFFERENT TYPES OF INGREDIENTS

A standard cup measure of a dry or solid ingredient will vary in weight depending on the type of ingredient. A standard cup of liquid is the same volume for any type of liquid. Use the following chart when converting standard cup measures to grams (weight) or milliliters (volume).

Standard Cup	Fine Powder (ex. flour)	Grain (ex. rice)	Granular (ex. sugar)	Liquid Solids (ex. butter)	Liquid (ex. milk)
1	140 g	150 g	190 g	200 g	240 ml
¾	105 g	113 g	143 g	150 g	180 ml
⅔	93 g	100 g	125 g	133 g	160 ml
½	70 g	75 g	95 g	100 g	120 ml
⅓	47 g	50 g	63 g	67 g	80 ml
¼	35 g	38 g	48 g	50 g	60 ml
⅛	18 g	19 g	24 g	25 g	30 ml

USEFUL EQUIVALENTS FOR LIQUID INGREDIENTS BY VOLUME

¼ tsp					=	1 ml	
½ tsp					=	2 ml	
1 tsp					=	5 ml	
3 tsp	=	1 tbls		½ fl oz	=	15 ml	
	2 tbls	=	⅛ cup	= 1 fl oz	=	30 ml	
	4 tbls	=	¼ cup	= 2 fl oz	=	60 ml	
	5 ⅓ tbls	=	⅓ cup	= 3 fl oz	=	80 ml	
	8 tbls	=	½ cup	= 4 fl oz	=	120 ml	
	10 ⅔ tbls	=	⅔ cup	= 5 fl oz	=	160 ml	
	12 tbls	=	¾ cup	= 6 fl oz	=	180 ml	
	16 tbls	=	1 cup	= 8 fl oz	=	240 ml	
	1 pt	=	2 cups	= 16 fl oz	=	480 ml	
	1 qt	=	4 cups	= 32 fl oz	=	960 ml	
				= 33 fl oz	=	1000 ml	= 1 liter

USEFUL EQUIVALENTS FOR DRY INGREDIENTS BY WEIGHT
(To convert ounces to grams, multiply the number of ounces by 30.)

1 oz	=	¹⁄₁₆ lb	=	30 g
4 oz	=	¼ lb	=	120 g
8 oz	=	½ lb	=	240 g
12 oz	=	¾ lb	=	360 g
16 oz	=	1 lb	=	480 g

USEFUL EQUIVALENTS FOR LENGTH

(To convert inches to centimeters, multiply the number of inches by 2.5.)

1 in				= 2.5 cm		
6 in	=	½ ft		= 15 cm		
12 in	=	1 ft		= 30 cm		
36 in	=	3 ft	= 1 yd	= 90 cm		
40 in				= 100 cm	= 1 m

USEFUL EQUIVALENTS FOR COOKING/OVEN TEMPERATURES

	Fahrenheit	Celsius	Gas Mark
Freeze Water	32° F	0° C	
Room Temperature	68° F	20° C	
Boil Water	212° F	100° C	
Bake	325° F	160° C	3
	350° F	180° C	4
	375° F	190° C	5
	400° F	200° C	6
	425° F	220° C	7
	450° F	230° C	8
Broil			Grill

recipe index